Collective bargaining

What you always wanted to know
about trade unions and never dared to ask

Clive Jenkins and Barrie Sherman

Routledge & Kegan Paul
London, Henley and Boston

First published in 1977
by Routledge & Kegan Paul Ltd
39 Store Street,
London WC1E 7DD,
Broadway House,
Newtown Road,
Henley-on-Thames,
Oxon RG9 1EN and
9 Park Street,
Boston, Mass. 02108, USA
Set in Monotype Modern No. 7
by Kelly and Wright, Bradford-on-Avon, Wiltshire
and printed in Great Britain by
Lowe & Brydone Ltd

British Library Cataloguing in Publication Data

Jenkins, Clive

Collective bargaining
1. Collective bargaining – Great Britain
I. Title II. Sherman, Barrie
331.89'0941   HD6664   77–30044

ISBN 0-7100 8690-3
ISBN 0-7100 8691-1   Pbk

Contents

Introduction

In a mixed economy collective bargaining is about collective relations. The unions are the pistons in modifying these by their work in the market place.

A bargain can be defined as a contract struck between two or more parties, or a purchase where the cost is below market price or expectations of price. The former describes a collective bargaining situation, the latter is what collective bargaining hopes to stop an employer obtaining for his own profit.

The employer–employee or, as British law put it for so long, the master–servant relationship is one of acute imbalance. The employer possesses the economic power. The right of hire and fire, remuneration levels, working hours, work practices, indeed all facets of life at the work-place have been at the disposal of and under the control of the employer in a society such as ours.

This is now changing under the impact of union opinion and power which has stimulated supportive legislation but employers have capital or wealth; workers have a wage or income. In both present and potential economic terms a single employee confronting a single employer is like taking a watering-can to a Hiroshima fire. As the production process has become more capital intensive and concerns become larger to manage; as the growth of joint stock companies gives way to the growth of conglomerates, so the individual employees whether 'white-collared' staff or 'blue-collared' manual employees become more remote and isolated from their employer. When industrialisation started the employer often knew all employees by name; the entrepreneur not only boasted of his paternalism he often believed it and felt himself wounded if his workers brought in outsiders to disrupt the 'family' circle. Although this argument lingers on today (although for totally different

1

reasons in different circumstances in companies such as IBM, Michelin or some insurance companies) most workers cannot identify with their employing management nor the management with the workers – although they claim to. Given this estrangement it is a natural consequence for collective bargaining to take place on a strength-in-numbers or knowledge basis.

If you feel unwell you visit a doctor; if you have a toothache you visit a dentist; if you are involved in litigation you visit a solicitor; if collective bargaining needs to be done, workers approach a trade union. We live in the age of the professional and in the case of trade unions this applies to not only the negotiators but also to their research, legal and educational staffs.

In addition, there are bodies which take part in collective bargaining but which also have qualifying and disciplinary functions such as the nurses and professions supplementary to medicine in the National Health Service which at present negotiate within the Whitley Council framework. There is also a dwindling group of in-house Staff Associations, many of them in the finance sector. The small numbers of persons who joined the bogus and fragile 'new' associations which were encouraged by the Heath Government's Industrial Relations Act 1971 mainly failed to secure negotiating rights, went into decline and may be eliminated from this study as they do not form a significant part of the United Kingdom's industrial relations apparatus.

The only significant non-TUC collective bargaining activity (outside of the Whitley system) is on a numerically tiny scale. The First Division Association (senior civil servants), some school-masters, and a few chief officers in local government along with managers in the steel industry. There are also a handful of unions in the small General Confederation of Trade Unions and some newer management oriented staff associations none of which have made much impact.

Other bodies such as doctors' and dentists' associations, judges, senior nationalised industry personnel and Members of Parliament have their salaries set by Review Body procedures and play no part in collective bargaining as such.

It is not merely a tired cliché to state that a trade union is the sum of its members. Its power stems from this sum; the skills of the professional negotiators are supplementary and are superimposed. There are more than ten million men and women in trades unions affiliated to the Trades Union Congress. If one assumed that they represent average families then 61 per cent of the entire population of the United Kingdom have their incomes determined by collective bargaining and many of the remainder are pensioners whose occupational pensions were a subject of negotiations in the past, or even currently.

So while these other methods exist for determining rewards, collective bargaining is the almost universal method of arriving at a wage and may soon be so for pensions as well. It is not, as old-fashioned politicians suggest from time to time, operated on behalf of a small sectional interest – rather it tends to operate *against* such an interest on behalf of a large majority.

Because of the concept of collectivity the membership of a trade union must, in any individual situation, display a cohesiveness not always found in British society. It is this solidarity which both gives the additional strength and brings the opprobrium from the media most of which, of course, is still proprietorial. If a man or woman refuses to take industrial action when fellow workmates do, refuses to join a union in a closed-shop situation, or leaves a union, his heroism is assured in print. If their trade union attempts to take disciplinary action against such a member his martyrdom ranks with that of St Sebastian. Contrast this attitude with the treatment of armed service deserters, MPs who defy a three-line Whip or indeed dissident members of an exclusive club. The interesting point is that these employees have never foregone increases negotiated for them by a trade union nor do they forego the historic increases. In such situations a person who refuses to join or leaves a trade union, or refuses to lose short-term income is getting a higher real wage than those who have made his wage levels possible. In the first two cases the employee does not pay union subscriptions and in the latter accepts the fruit of the sacrifices of time made by work-fellows without personal financial sacrifice. In other walks of life those who demand benefits without participation are viewed unfavourably and it is not unnatural that this is also the case in a trade union context, but more sharply.

The scope of collective bargaining has changed out of all recognition since 1945. Classes of employees who felt they were individually capable of handling wage negotiations have been disabused of this idea in the harshest possible ways by successive Governmental incomes policies and because of the relative losses of incomes these employees have taken to joining trades unions by the hundreds of thousands. A second change is the extension of topics upon which a trade union feels competent to negotiate. At one time wages, hours of work, and in some cases work conditions, constituted the entire range of activities. The manual workers' unions have extended this while, the 'white-collar' unions which started from a higher plateau of fringe benefits have extended it far further into a 'remuneration package'. This includes pensions, overtime, holidays, car allowances, discretionary loans and mortgages, trust funds, and a host of compensatory allowances.

Yet another change in collective bargaining is in its sophistication. As unions at last managed to gain a larger measure of income equitability, so employers hired more expert personnel to negotiate with them. The preparation and advocacy of arbitration cases and evidence to investigators, committees and tribunals has demanded a higher level of awareness and ingenuity more commonly associated with the Bar than with trade union negotiators. This was particularly demonstrated at the so-called 'self defence' cases at the now-repealed National Industrial Relations Court and no doubt will be a necessary and acceptable burden in the operation of the various procedures within the Advisory, Conciliation and Arbitration Service and those set up under the Employee Protection Legislation, the Equal Pay Act, and the Sex Discrimination Act.

The vertical integration of certain industries has made one settlement in isolation almost an impossibility. The effect, either the negotiation or the settlement, reverberates through that sector of the economy. Negotiations have become an art form, company or union statements are written and read with the zeal of mediaeval textual analysts.

Keynsian economics, or at least what passes for them now, have also changed the character of collective bargaining which now has to be anticipatory. Since 1945 successive governments have tried to affect the economy more directly than hitherto and when they have failed have nevertheless taken responsibility for it. Balance of payments problems have dictated the infamous stop–go policies of governments using fiscal, monetary and other budgetary devices. The growth of deficit budgeting has accounted for most of the increase in domestic public expenditure and governments have successfully tried to bribe employers to move into depressed areas. The result has been that in major negotiations (particularly in the public sector) the Government has been an overt third party and in the smaller ones Government policies have sought to dictate the outcome of negotiations in often a very precise and precedent-setting manner.

A decisive change has been made by the imposition of the law. This has been in two distinct forms; legislation which has had an indirect impact on collective bargaining and that which has had a direct effect. The 1971 Industrial Relations Act had a marked effect in a negative way: it generated a ground swell of opinion for real reform. The unions quite rapidly abandoned their old resistance to any laws at all in favour of laws which caught up with such rights as other unions have long enjoyed in Northern Europe. The 1973 counter inflation legislation also had an enormous direct effect on bargaining, as has the 1975/6/7 Social Contract.

The new laws and projected laws on Social Security, Fair Trading, Company Law, Health and Safety, Discrimination, Pensions and Industrial Democracy and all enactments on economic matters will have a major influence on trends. It remains to be seen quite what effect the European Economic Community legislation will have. We can see the impact on food prices and balance of payments both of which influence bargainers and government but the mobility of labour, European procedure agreements, Works Council proposals along with harmonisation of health and social programmes will all play a part and the creation of the European company will reverberate whether or not the UK remains in the EEC in the long term.

A trade union has thus to cope with a mass of legislative changes as well as with employers who, by and large, are still in a posture of institutionalised opposition. The individual union member cannot cope with this infrastructure as adequately as the employer, the more so because it is changing at an incomprehensibly rapid pace. The anti-inflation legislation, for example, spawned a green paper, a white paper and a statutory instrument within the space of four months in 1972–3, each of which was marginally yet significantly different, yet the legislation lasted only for nine months. How could individual employees do their own jobs all week, master the legislation and also negotiate on their own behalf? The simple answer is that they could not and did not.

Each individual trade union has the opportunity to influence overall trade union policy; each individual member has the opportunity to be elected to the highest offices within the union. It is incumbent in the British tradition for the individual to accept a majority decision. British Parliamentary democracy is founded firmly on a strong government 'winner take all' principle and this has been accepted by the trade union movement. The position in the unions is different however because they are *permanent* organisations. Every agreement they conclude is linked to the last deal – and to the next one. So the argument always goes on.

The overwhelming majority of trade union members in Britain realise this very clearly. They are members because they know they cannot do the job for themselves and are prepared to contribute to have it done for them. The British public may or may not be the most politically sophisticated in the world – there are gaps. But they have intuitively and by experience recognised that the Continental Works Council and the Company-based staff association stereotypes are too hopelessly compromised in internally-locked situations for them to be effective. All bargainers must be linked with the outside movement: this gives the negotiators the strength that they need to match the employers' economic power.

The trade union negotiates a settlement with an employer within a framework of a procedural agreement between the parties. This agreement and the settlement superimposed on it forms the master contract, each individual contract of employment still having a legal standing and relevance. The individual's contract of employment is strangely wide including as it legally does all restrictions or licences which are posted for general consumption. An unprotested notice on a factory wall warning that protective headgear must be worn then forms part of an individual's contract. In this respect the master contract negotiated in collective bargaining bears a close resemblance to other aspects of an individual's contract of employment. The master contract supplements the individual one in defining the total conditions under which an employee works *vis-à-vis* his employer. Collective bargaining sets the levels at which these conditions are pitched by a process known as negotiations.

The concept of negotiating has already occurred several times in this book and will pervade the entire thesis. It is the central function of a trade union. The union's collectivity and coherence merely provide the basic background to effective negotiating; as Bevan once remarked, 'I will not go into the debating chamber naked' meaning negotiations must take place on as equal a ranking of strength as can be achieved if they are to be meaningful.

Negotiating is a skilled procedure which leads to a settlement, often but not necessarily by compromise between the parties. Negotiations must not be confused with consultations, a distinction which backward employers sometimes seek to blur. The average consultations imply that a draft decision has been taken and that other interested parties only then acquire a status to discuss the matter. This has been especially true of industrial relations in the field of pensions and was seen in its most perfected form in the meetings between the TUC and the Government over Phases II and III Incomes Policy in 1973. All that these meetings achieved was to confer a form of legitimacy on the final outcome; lip service was paid to democracy but the entrenched attitude of 'thank you for coming we will bear your ideas in mind' was highly visible.

Negotiating is far removed from this tokenism; it is a reality. It is two parties aiming at least at equal strength, each with a pre-arranged bargaining position sitting around tables and finally settling on a position which satisfies both sides. It is a short-term procedure, a reactive procedure, but it is a living dynamic procedure which is open ended to the future. It is based on traditional British political life where the party in power often prudently hesitates to maximise its use of that power because it fears retribution when its opposition becomes the majority party; the result is a compromise. On the basis that the exception proves the rule the Heath Government in 1970 and 1971 ignored this premise but subsequently had to reverse or ignore its original policies at great political expense, the loss of its leaders, and finally perhaps its life as a major party.

A journalist once described the procedures in collective bargaining as a Western 'Japanese tea ceremony'. By this, she meant that the ritualisation not only of procedures, but postures mainly intended for the media, were becoming irrelevant. She might also have mentioned the ritual before two Samurai swordsmen fight; it could have been more apt. There is some point to her observation in that certain stages must be proceeded with in the normal run of events and they may be formalities, both sides realising that negotiations will only be concluded in the later stages of the designated game plan. The public utterances in both the press and broadcasting are generally a deliberate appeal to public opinion but have limited effect; for example in 1972 the hospital workers in dispute had immense public sympathy but did not achieve their objectives. However, they then regrouped in an entirely predictable way. There is no direct correlation between the public's perception of the 'rightness' of the claim and the success of the negotiations, although it must be stated that to have opinion on your side when Ministers are the paymasters is always welcome.

In the same way a persuasive presentation of a claim cannot always be said to be a total criterion of success. We would all like to think that we live in a world where reasoned argument wins the day.

If this were so Britain would be a far better place to live in than it is at present. It would also be gratifying for a well-documented, agreed and reasoned case for a claim to win the day – on its own. In 1971 a research unit prepared a long, reasoned and sophisticated claim for the manual workers in their wage round in the automative industry. It was not perfect, but it was a radical departure from historical precedents in manufacturing industry. An eleven-week strike followed. In 1972 a group of Scottish engineering workers presented a claim for a substantial pay increase in these words, 'Johnny wants a biscuit and he wants it now.' A settlement acceptable to both sides followed immediately. Although neither occurrence should be viewed as typical it does show that sophistication may not always be the most efficacious therapy in industrial relations: power matters too.

In the last analysis, negotiations are between parties with entrenched positions who both have something to lose and something to gain. There have been many occasions when the employer has refused to compromise and industrial action has followed. There are immeasurably more cases where a consensus position has been reached with neither side losing anything but to the satisfaction of both sides. Arbitration has settled other cases.

This short book is concerned with the mechanisms involved in collective bargaining in modern Britain. It takes into account recent legislation and the direct and indirect effects this can have on bargaining. It looks at technology and the changing patterns of the British work force. It seeks to trace the stages of bargaining in differing circumstances and industries through the labyrinth (carefully avoiding the Minotaur) of procedures and courts. It examines the law in relation to collective bargaining identifying the constraints and the use of the legal processes in a trade union's work. Industrial relations, like companies, are supranational and this growing phenomenon is examined.

The book is one of explanation and technique and is intended to show how a trade union actually operates in a simple way. Some of the techniques are novel, others are workaday, some of the procedures are unusual, most are standard though widely misreported.

Although there are more than ten million bona fide trades union members in Britain, the lack of understanding of basic trade union work is at a baffling level. This is partly the fault of the trade union movement in not deliberately explaining its services to the public and partly partisan reporting from which one might believe that the sole functions of a union were 'kangaroo courts', sending people to Coventry and violent picketing. This is patently absurd as this book shows. The limits to which both sides will usually go to avoid a confrontation using procedural methods are extraordinary. Above all this is intended to be a guide to collective bargaining for those involved in it and those wishing to learn about it.

Chapter 1

The failures of Conservative legislation affecting collective bargaining

'Curiouser and curiouser' – Lewis Carroll

We all live with interventionist legislation. It affects us literally from the moment of birth, with registration requirements, through to death, with certification, autopsies and coroners' courts. In between times there is no activity in life free from legal restraints; food, choice of leisure or reading material, sexual gratification, even the basic drives are the subject of laws. We are told that this way lies freedom and freedom from legal restraint brings licence at the least, anarchy at the worst. Industrial relations have not escaped from this all-embracing theory and its legal frameworks; indeed it can be argued that in direct form they are more constrained than almost all other activities or that, indirectly, legislative impact has recently shaped the form of collective bargaining in Britain decisively.

The 1971 legislation

Prior to 1971 there were many acts that affected the legal entity and responsibility of trade unions in Britain. The Trade Union Act 1871 and the 1875 Trade Union Act Amendment Act were the lynch pins with the 1896 Friendly Societies Act providing registration provisions. In addition the 1906 Trades Dispute Act created the framework within which a trade union could legally operate or rather – in a peculiarly British way – could operate outside of it. In effect the British unions, uniquely for developed countries, were exempted from the legal consequences of certain acts which would otherwise be actionable. But it is argued that this simply diminished the drive for *affirmative* rights for unions. These Acts have now been repealed in their entirety along with the partial or full repeal of a further fifteen Acts, and amendments to a further twelve Acts. The large body of case-law built up on these various Acts, is now no longer needed. The whole bundle was replaced by the 1971 Industrial Relations Act – all 186 pages of it which has itself been amended by the latest repeals and substituting Acts.

Of all recent legislation affecting collective bargaining this Act was potentially the most disruptive, but fortunately a majority of both sides of industry realised the dangers of its full implementation and ignored it by tacit agreement. The maverick individuals, unrecognised quasi-unions or companies which sought legal remedies under the Act heaped embarrassments onto the Government as industrial relations in those situations worsened considerably. On the solitary occasion the Government intervened, using the Act for a secret ballot of railwaymen, the union leaderships were overwhelmingly vindicated and a dispute situation hardened; the legislation proved decisively counter-productive.

Having made this point, the Industrial Relations Act had an impact on trade unions, if only in a negative sense. Precautions had to be taken to protect the memberships against its effects. A second point is that in some sectors the act spawned a collection of quasi-unions, which used it to create a significant nuisance in the 'recognition' fields, both to employers and established trade unions by claiming a right to splinter existing representative bodies. It now seems quite remarkable that the traditional trade unions which deregistered at the call of the TUC were legally stripped of that title and became 'organisations of workers' while the upstarts who registered then had the sole legal claim to be called 'trade unions'. When the Government sat down and talked with the TUC affiliates it was, strictly speaking, not meeting a single 'trade union'. The late Lord Feather while General Secretary of the Trades Union Congress said to one of the authors 'if this goes on much longer we will have to call ourselves the Congress of Organisations of Workers – but I do not like the initials!'

The Industrial Relations Act 1971 arose out of a Conservative Party document entitled 'Fair Deal at Work' which owed a debt to an earlier publication of the lawyers in the Conservative Inns of Court Associations entitled 'A Giant's Strength'. It was sold to the public in a curious, disingenuous and dangerous way. The argument went as follows. Industrial relations were anarchic, unofficial strikes were rampant, something needed to be done, ergo, the Industrial Relations Act. There has always been an argument for some form of structural and legislative reform. Lord Donovan's Royal Commission on Trades Unions and Employers' Organisations made many such recommendations – nearly all of which were ignored by the Conservative Government of 1970. The philosophy behind their Act was that of discipline and centralisation; the philosophy of

Donovan was to devolve power to the shop floor; thus the Industrial Relations Act totally contradicted the only authoritative study on British trade unions in this century. Of course, the misconception was that there existed an oppressed silent majority waiting for its shackles to be struck off. Historically, the contrary was true. The unorganised had begun to look with admiration at the gains made by unions. The 1971 Act simply gave a platform to the traditional eccentric English litigant.

Let us examine that government's arguments more closely. If something was wrong then patently remedial action was necessary but what was not necessary was the Industrial Relations Act. This Act was not a serious attempt to solve industrial relations problems but a political attempt to create an imbalance leaning dramatically in favour of the employers: this could not last because it rested on the hotly-contested proposition that the employer knew best and had some social superiority.

In hindsight the Act proved to be a watershed for union attitudes. By bringing the law into each single facet of their own activities the unions realised that there was a possibility of using the law to gain affirmative rights. The Industrial Relations Act thus had a catalytic effect. It also had the effect of training some union officials in the concept of the law and persuading some unions to improve their back-up legal and research facilities.

Before 1971 the trade union movement had strenuously opposed legislative interference (as they saw it) in their activities. By 1974, however, they were not only prepared to accept the Trade Union and Labour Relations Act (TULRA) which was in essence simply the repeal legislation, but actually to fight for the Employment Protection Act and other succouring legislation. There is, indeed, still a minority school of thought within the trade union movement which believes the law has no part to play and that industrial relations are best left to traditional methods. The majority, however, now realise that certain rights and standards are best laid down within a legal framework. A caveat must, however, be entered in that it is very difficult to draft legislation which gives precise effect to Parliamentary intent, a difficulty which is shown in detail by the definition of 'independent union' in the TULRA.

It is worth while briefly running through the main features of the Industrial Relations Act so as to compare them with those of the Employment Protection Act provoked by them and described in chapter eleven. All unions had to register. The criteria governing registration were complex but revolved around the Rule books of trade unions. Although the majority of TUC affiliates would have had little difficulty in meeting these criteria (had they chosen to do so), company oriented staff associations and other quasi-unions had no such difficulties and proliferated in numbers if not in paying membership.* Registration conferred many privileges, both financial and practical. A Registered Union could get tax relief on its investment income, had access to the Industrial Relations Court, could call strikes and negotiate Agency Shops (where every employee joined the recognised union or paid the equivalent of a subscription to an agreed charity). By and large TUC affiliates did not register as a result of a TUC Congress decision and it is a matter of history that this act of apparent self-denial virtually made the Act unworkable. The reason was that the Act could not exercise much degree of control over non-registered bodies and thus practical considerations added to the more psychological functions of a focus of opposition. The initiators of the Act got this point politically wrong.

Several new ideas and new terminology hit the British industrial relations scene, most of them borrowed from the United States. The first was the 'unfair industrial practice', which sounds as though industrial relations are a sort of cricket and there were a host of these alleged. Agreements were deemed to be legally enforceable unless a disclaimer was specifically added. This annoyed both unions and management almost more than any other clause as agreements are very rarely wittingly broken by either side. As a result, a disclaimer was invariably added which gave agreements the same status, only written instead of verbal, as those struck on the Stock Exchange.

Two other US concepts which were filched were the 'Agency Shop' and the 'sole bargaining agency'. These were intended to replace the traditional pre or post-entry closed shop. Section 7 of the Act outlawed the closed shop but both sides of industry virtually ignored this;† only the odd plaintiffs, such as a Mr Goad, kept the issue alive. The Agency Shop, as noted earlier, allowed non-union members to either pay contributions to the union without becoming a member or a 'conscientious objector' could pay the money to charity instead. The sole bargaining agency was very different. In this case a union was awarded, by an employer, or by the Industrial Relations Court, negotiating rights to the exclusion of all other unions. The major problem in this instance was that some employers awarded these rights to staff associations which they themselves dominated and financed thus effectively cutting off their staff from

---

* Although one major non-TUC union the Institute of Professional Civil Servants abandoned its plan to register when too many changes were demanded in its Rule Book. The Institute finally joined the TUC in 1976.

† Except for the public sector when managements were under direct Ministerial control. However the ranks mainly held firm there as well.

real collective bargaining. The Act buttressed their anti-union strategy.

The Act also created the National Industrial Relations Court and vastly expanded the Industrial Tribunal system, whilst appropriating (and thus destroying the credibility of) the Commission on Industrial Relations. The media concentrated on the Court and its President Sir John Donaldson in such controversial cases as the dockers (the Pentonville Five) who went to gaol and were rescued by the Official Solicitor, the Con-Mech case, the swingeing impost on the Engineering Union's political fund and the eccentric litigants. There were, however, many other cases where TUC affiliates were dragged in by staff associations and others to defend their bargaining rights. ASTMS officers alone spent hundreds of days preparing for, or at, the Court, always defending themselves with back-up only from their expert professional and legal advisers.

The Industrial Relations Act also created the idea of unfair dismissal which has, of course, survived the Act and been expanded. These cases were heard at the Tribunals which, because the TUC refused to nominate members, handed down decisions without sympathy and without reasonable compensation. But trade union officials also represented their members, thus building up expertise. The much publicised trivial cases at the Tribunals are usually taken by non-union individuals with grudges.

The Industrial Relations Act thus forced unions and their officials to gain experience in unfamiliar areas; to cope with Draconian and restrictive laws thus digging deep into their reserves of ingenuity; to invest time and money which, in other circumstances, could have been more wisely applied and finally, to accustom unions to the notion of legislation. However, the shock effect led to detailed consideration of reform.

The aftermath

When in 1974 a Labour Government was elected, it pledged itself to the repeal of the Act. But to do so not only required a repealing Act but ancillary legislation to give unions a legal basis which had been swept away by the passing of the 1971 Act. Once this had been realised and the unfair dismissal legislation had been amended and re-enacted, it was only a short step to press for specific industrial relations legislation which would provide effective rights and provide an environment within which the whole practice of union–management relations could be undertaken. This embracing of the legal process was started by the Donovan Report and refined in discussions and seminars after this report, but it took the Industrial

Relations Act to provoke union leaders and their lawyers into positive action. Equally, both the public and Parliament had become accustomed to legal involvement in industrial relations. Thus time and conditions conspired to create the Employment Protection Act. We shall look at this Act in some detail later in the book, but before that we return to the main burden of this chapter, which is collective bargaining and legislation.

Common Market considerations

Although the Employment Protection Act was intended directly to affect collective bargaining much other legislation has a peripheral or sectoral effect. Probably the most important of all recent developments was the European Communities Act which allowed Britain to sign the Treaty of Accession to the Common Market.

Trade unions created the Labour Party and the Labour Movement as a whole has always been political in a Parliament-orientated sense. Unions seek the aid of Members of Parliament not only on broad matters of policy, but also for lobbying in specific industrial disputes. Some trade unions simply provide a financial sponsorship for MPs; others have Parliamentary committees which meet regularly to discuss such problems with the permanent union officials. Others pay a retaining fee to MPs who act as advisers. Legislation is the foundation of our society and it is not unnatural for a trade union to wish to change, lobby on, or instigate legislative measures which it believes are desirable for its membership.

Since 1 January 1973 this component of union work has diminished in importance. Entry to the European Economic Community brought in its wake such a loss of sovereignty that it is possible to envisage a future Government as having abdicated. It is complicated and difficult for an individual trade union to lobby directly in the EEC for two reasons. The elected representatives are confined to the European Parliament which has little power, and the executive arm, the Commission, apart from the unwieldy and time-consuming Economic and Social Committee has few specific apertures for trade unions except on the bipartite employer–employee committees, and some advisory bodies. Some of these committees represent an attempt to start Common Market-wide procedures and conditions of service agreements. The consultative bodies include the Economic and Social Committee and all of its associated sub-committees and others including iron and steel, coal and energy. At any one of these the impact of British unions is limited by the advisory-only status, by the fact that union experts are often not allowed and there exist limitations on substitute delegates. The practice is that a trade union must, if it wishes to influence events, exert pressure on its national institutions and these will then act in Brussels (see chapter ten).

Legislation of varying degrees of effectiveness has been made in Brussels affecting the everyday lives of the British people, both at work and at leisure. Having taken a draft decision on worker participation in management the EEC effectively precluded the trade union movement from having any say in the formulation; the discussion is now about means in the rest of the EEC, with Britain holding its own internal inquiries (see chapter eleven). Qualifications, whether of general degrees or specific professional standards, are to be 'harmonised' – a necessity if the free mobility of labour is to mean anything. A trade union such as ASTMS, with a high percentage of qualified members, is still seeking adequate methods of representing their interests in this important matter, which will change the face of their labour market and thus ultimately their salaries and security.

These are two examples of a specific problem, the overall political strategies are even less accessible to trade unions. The Common Agricultural Policy, the Iron and Steel quotas and pricing mechanisms, monetary union, defence agreements, aid to or boycotts of other countries, all of these most important decisions will be taken by the bureaucracy of the Nine without an effective checking voice from the trade unions. Yet each of these will affect the members of unions in bargaining situations. It is a situation unique in British history. EEC legislation will be binding, will have to be learned and acted upon by British unions, yet the unions and their members are virtually disenfranchised in this respect.

Sex Discrimination

Equal pay and equal opportunity for women in Britain is one area where the trade union movement has been historically both voluble and ineffective at one and the same time. The Equal Pay Act was implemented in December 1975, a full four and a half years after enactment. Even now, however, equal pay is still not a universal condition within Britain. The Act lays down the rules and regulations regarding equal pay, defines it and lays down the remedies for non-implementation. The Act, however, is far from perfect and trade unions will have the responsibility of seeing that the provisions of the Act are adhered to and that the many loopholes that exist are not exploited. Two large Employers' Federations have given their members advice on evading both the spirit and intent of the Act, quite legally of course. If unions are to defend their members, both men and women, such avoidance of responsibilities will have to be countered in the industrial relations amphitheatre. This Act will probably prove a bonanza to consultancies which specialise in job evaluation. The concept of 'equal value' is one which can only be handled on a job evaluation or marginal economic framework and as the former is the more practical, one supposes that this will be in common use. The trade unions will have to master all the evaluation techniques (each consultancy uses its own) or will have to adopt a technique and arrange for it to be used by each employer.

Even if this is possible the problems for the trade union side do not end. Not only is the concept of 'jobs of equal value' one which permits of differing interpretations but the Act states that if the differences between a man and a woman's job are 'of practical importance in relation to terms and conditions of employment' the Act need not apply. In general terms the more imprecise a piece of legislation, the larger the coach and the more horses which can be driven through it. On this principle it could be that few, if any women, will get equal pay because of this section; a whole Lord Mayor's procession could pass through with ease. The Engineering Employers' Federation believes that job evaluation will minimise their costs by the expedient of evaluating skills in favour of men, e.g., physical strength will have a higher weighting than manual dexterity, night work be adjudged more valuable than day work and so on.

The Sex Discrimination Act 1975 is intended to be a supplement to the equal pay legislation. Basically, it quite correctly is based on the premise that equal pay without equality of opportunity cannot solve many fundamental problems. From a social point of view the use of the new Equal Opportunities Commission to investigate cases of discrimination on the grounds of gender or marital status in recruitment, education and in the workplace must thoroughly be welcomed. Equally, the extension of unfair dismissal on discriminatory grounds and the use of industrial tribunals must be seen as a step in the right direction. Nevertheless, both Acts have gaps, especially in regard to social benefits and pensions and neither Act can be declared to be a success until the results of the tribunal references are properly evaluated as the first seem to contain the seeds of future discord. Trade unions, especially those in the white-collar sector, will undoubtedly have to report abuses and make representations to both the Commission and Industrial Tribunals.

By and large, these are welcome pieces of legislation but may neither go far enough nor deep enough. As they stand they will have an impact on collective bargaining and trade unions will have to master them to get the best settlements for their women members, and to ensure that women, at long last, gain access to the sorts of jobs that have been denied them for so long.

General legislation

Collective bargaining includes within itself the protection of the individual's rights at work, guaranteed by both their collective agreement and the Contracts of Employment Act 1972. The Act was to some extent an adjunct to the Industrial Relations Act and involved the industrial tribunals and the Act itself from time to time, and sections 19–21 and Schedule 2 to this Act have been repealed. It is essential for trade union negotiators to know the sections on notice periods, the references to Industrial Tribunals, the form in which contracts are set out and result in contractual terms of changes in the terms of employment, and which categories of workers they exclude. Negotiators must have this information if they are to represent their members in the best possible manner.

Other recent legislation affects trade unions in varying degrees. The Social Security Pensions Act lays down new minimum criteria for Occupational Pensions and these must be known by any union with ambitions to negotiating pensions. These will be dealt with later in the book. Both the Local Government Re-organisation Act and the National Health Service Re-organisation Act had a significant impact on unions with membership in these areas. These latter two Acts will affect the salaries, working conditions, promotion prospects and job security of all those who work in Local Government and the National Health Service. The effect on collective bargaining is thus considerable and is compounded by the fact that in both cases the Acts have changed the employing body. It is interesting to note that although the employers will change in the NHS it is anticipated that the existing mechanism will remain. This entails the 'Whitley system' with no official procedure agreements. This cumbersome, impenetrably bureaucratic system is now under criticism for its lack of accountability and its sheer slowness – which may not survive the enquiry completed at the end of 1976 by Lord McCarthy for the Secretary of State.

The Industry Act 1975 affects unions in redundancy situations, which are, unfortunately, a feature of collective bargaining in the society in which we find ourselves. Unions can now, in theory at least, approach either the National Enterprise Board or the Department of Industry for aid to be given to their ailing employers. The Immigration Act 1971 could have a marked effect on collective bargaining in certain areas of Britain by creating a low-wage, captive, non-patrial workforce and thus forcing down other salaries (much in the same way as employers have used women). The effects of the Act in this respect have been reinforced by the Government decision to back-date the sanctions against illegal immigration and thus hand a second constraint against the worker to the employer.

All the above laws impinge on, or constrain, collective bargaining in Britain and all have been enacted within the last three years. General legislation affects collective bargaining as it affects all of life, but in an indirect way. Local Authority expenditure, with its impact on rents and rates, affects the consumption patterns of workers in that the money available after deductions and essential (inelastic) purchases has changed. By the same token, changes in the fiscal system alter disposable income or, in the case of indirect taxation, real income. As both of these factors are important in making a case for increases in remuneration the impact on collective bargaining is substantial, thus each year's Finance Act affects basic trade union work and almost all Acts from consumer protection to a private members Act on Employment Agencies must be considered, dissected, absorbed, analysed and, in the final reckoning, incorporated into procedural changes.

Conservative Party incomes policy

One important law now overtaken by two General Elections has been left until the last as its importance, in practical terms, outweighed even that of the Industrial Relations Act. It is, of course, the 1972–3 Counter-Inflation policy and Act. The Counter Inflation policy came into being on 7 November 1972 as Phase I; 'The Freeze' and Phase II, instituting the Prices Commission and Pay Board, came into force on 1 April 1973.

This book is not intended to debate the merits or otherwise of this particular form of prices and incomes control, nor indeed the philosophy behind all such policies. The electorate has rudely rejected the theory of legal penalties for non-observance, the apparatus and the politicians involved. But those who believe there has been unfettered free collective bargaining in the last decade should recall the following legislation. There were Prices and Incomes Acts in 1966, 1967, 1968 and lasting until early 1970; Counter Inflation policies and Acts in 1972, 1973 and early 1974 and a coercive 'Social Contract' in 1975, 1976 and 1977. Thus, in the eleven years from 1966 only 1971 was technically free from Government legislative interference in the collective bargaining mechanism. In this period only trade unions showing the greatest

ingenuity, the greatest determination and the greatest understanding of the legislation have been able to provide their members
with a service worthy of the name; this has been reflected in their
membership growth or decline. The £6 limit of 1975, probably the
most successful of these policies, does not involve direct legal
constraints against unions, rather it is aimed at unions through the
intermediary of the employer. From November 1972 to April 1973
there was an absolute standstill in wages though not of remuneration, and it is possible to record hundreds of increases in this period
stemming from collective bargaining. This was followed by a
Green Paper (a consultative document), a White Paper, and finally
the Act itself dated 22 March 1973. These followed in rapid succession
and the changes in successive documents were radical especially
those between the Green and White Papers; unfortunately for
employees the latter changes from the White Paper to enactment
were of concessions to vested interests on prices and profits.

The Act itself was a piece of enabling legislation; the nuts and
bolts of the policy were contained in the Statutory Instrument which
laid down a rigid framework within which both the Prices and Pay
authorities had to operate. Its importance on collective bargaining
as a whole cannot be overestimated for, in theory, every bargain
had to be made within the Consultative Document criteria. In
practice most were, but as with all legislation, certain manipulations were undertaken to avoid or minimise the intent. The Act set
up the Pay Board, now abolished. There was clear philosophical
difference of emphasis between the 1966–70 Prices and Incomes
Board and the 1973 Pay Board and Prices Commission. The earlier
Board explicitly acknowledged that each wage-increase seeker was
also a consumer and recognised the complete interdependence of
prices and incomes, indeed the philosophy went further in
recognising that wages and salaries are merely the price in a labour
sale. The later legislation did not recognise this and it made an
overt distinction, dividing the economy into disparate sectors each
with their own separate and jostling criteria. An additional difference
is that the earlier legislation gave the National Board of Prices and
Incomes latitude in its decisions, and arranged for it to have a large
high-powered team, while the 1973 version had no function other
than to carry out strict government policy to the letter. In short,
whilst the first Board was an independent body the second two
boards were no more independent than a prisoner in an open
prison.

The demise of the Pay Board was not celebrated. It was barely
noticed, although the legislation laid down stringent procedures.
An increase for a group of over 1,000 workers had to be submitted

to the Pay Board for their prior approval and they had twelve weeks to decide as to whether the increase was allowable given the parameters of the Statutory Instrument. Employers of groups of workers between 100 and 999 who were applying for increases had to inform the Pay Board of the increase within one week of the increase being made. It was theoretically possible that the Board could not only vet such an increase, but, in the event of it having been paid for this period, to order the employees to repay the excess to the employer. Had the Board ever ordered this the resulting industrial chaos would have needed to be seen to be believed. Employers with under 100 workers in a group had to keep records of increases and these could be requisitioned by the Pay Board.

In practice nearly all employers contacted the Pay Board to ask if the settlement agreed with the trade union met the criteria and the Board offered its opinion. This was not the intention of the Act. Unsatisfactory employers used the Board as a reason why they could not meet their responsibilities and maintained incorrectly, that to offer more than the Board said it would allow would be illegal.

A very important point is that it became illegal to strike (or take industrial action short of a strike), in defiance of an Order. This itself ran counter to the Industrial Relations Act. An example of the misunderstanding was the situation at Chrysler UK in September 1973. A small group of electricians at the Coventry plant struck in furtherance of a claim (the substance of this claim had been promised in the 1972 negotiations). The Company publicly stated it would be illegal to meet the claim. If this were so, the EEPTU could have been fined up to £400 for their strike on summary conviction; they were not. In practice the claim could have been met, an Order issued, and the onus for the lack of satisfactory settlement placed firmly on the Pay Board; as it was, a crisis developed most unnecessarily. Lord Goodman seems originally to have fallen into the same error during the dispute between the Newspaper Proprietors' Association and the printing unions – this was privately rectified.

What emerges from this is that during Phase II it was necessary to persuade employers to eschew contacts with the Pay Board prior to a settlement.

When negotiating with an employer in this period the general tactic was to make the employer realise that it was in his interests to remunerate the staff adequately, distance him from the Statutory Instrument, and reach an accommodation satisfactory to both sides.

The Statutory Instrument covered all remuneration. The £1 + 4 per cent formula was well known but less well known were the lack of productivity provisions and the strict restrictions on overtime, holidays, hours of work and other elements in the salary package. Certain gaps existed and these were exploited, but the 1973 legislation learned a lot from the earlier attempts in closing such gaps.

Phase II interpolated itself between the management and unions in collective bargaining and this involved union negotiators knowing the Act and Statutory Instrument. Phase III followed Phase II along with a Pay Board report on anomalies aroused by Phase I of the policy. Collective bargaining is a skilled occupation. With the intrusion of such legislation it becomes an exercise in Machiavellian policies and only the unions with good, intelligent negotiators, backed up by a first-class research and legal service managed to offer their members an adequate service. They did, but the repressive legal framework was both offensive and farcically incapable of being operated.

Labour incomes policy

When, in July 1975, the Labour Government decided that the rate of inflation, running at roughly 26 per cent per year, could only be solved by restricting wage increases, they used the experiences and mistakes of the previous decade. Instead of a tightly-drawn series of regulations each of which carried a penalty if broken by the employees, the £6 limit was a simple concept with the minimum of detail. The flat-rate £6 per week increase had the advantages of first being seen to be advantageous to the lower paid (even if it completely upset established collectively bargained differentials) and second, that of being easily and comprehensively understood by all workers. This was reinforced by an anti-inflation propaganda unit with a £3 million budget which not only produced a pamphlet which was then circulated to every household in Britain, but also a series of advertisements in the national press.

The reasons why the £6 limit worked so effectively were complex. First, the trade unions themselves acquiesced, although a 1975 Congress decision on free collective bargaining was only defeated by a 6:4 ratio. Second, there was the simplicity and lack of punitive constraints. The theory was that if a wage bill rose by more than £6 per head on aggregate (including everything except existing productivity schemes) a private sector employer would not be able to get *any* price increases passed through the Price Commission. The system is thus voluntary in that any company can, if it wishes, pay more than the £6 but forego its revenue increases. However, if more than one industry or perhaps one large company did so and the fact was widely publicised, the Government would be forced to enact the punitive measures which were, in the event, held in reserve.

The policy initially was to be monitored by both the TUC and the CBI. However, as a practical measure this was dropped. A union such as ASTMS has over 5,000 different and separate basic primary negotiations each year and monitoring on this level for a body like the TUC is quite impossible. The monitoring was, however, not really needed. Despite some marginal inequalities (marginal in the total policy sense) such as the payment of increments in the public but not the private sector and London Allowance discrepancies, the policy went through unchallenged. The lack of detail was by far the strongest point. Nothing could be circumvented, because nothing was written. If a loophole was found the Department of Employment closed it because they were the sole arbiter.

The control over the public sector was simple. The Government controls its funds, either wholly or partially, and if the £6 limit were to be broken, the funds would not have been made up and in some cases presumably surcharges could be made. Behind the policy and contributing greatly to its success was the backing of the TUC, without this the probability was of a confrontation.

By the summer of 1976 'son of Social Contract' was under way. At the time of writing it is too soon to know whether this will be as successful as its progenitor. It suffers from the disadvantage that it is more complex. There is a minimum and maximum increase, £2.25 up to £4 per week and in between an increase of 5 per cent with the same unknown Department of Employment interpretations ready to block potential loopholes. This policy, passed overwhelmingly by a special TUC Congress is perhaps less likely to pass off so peaceably even if it ultimately runs its full course to August 1977.

There are many aggrieved employees whose differentials have been either reduced (in some instances totally eroded) during the first £6 policy whose relative position will, by mid-1977 probably prove intolerable. There are other groups which, by strangely inconsistent Department of Employment decisions, have had anomalies working against them and these will have to carry over for another full year, or are even being multiplied. These matters affect basically the skilled and white-collar sectors of the labour force.

However, a novel feature of the policy, which may ultimately expand, was the use by the Chancellor of the Exchequer in his Budget speech of tax concessions, if and only if the trade unions accepted the proposed wage restraint. This was, in British terms, a unique offer. It was also a very worrying one. It meant that the TUC was placed in a position, not of its own volition, of determining the tax allowances of the non-unionists in the workforce. It was a position in which, in public relations terms, the TUC could only lose by rejecting the offer even if, as we believe, that offer was derisory.

The tactic, however, succeeded in the short term. In the longer term it does two things. First, it demolishes the normal management agreement that one cannot bargain on net earnings, only gross ones. Second, it has made it clear to both union officials and members that their standard of living is determined by real, disposable income. That is to say, earnings less tax and national insurance contributions deflated by the Retail Price Index. ASTMS has used this approach for the past few years in major claims with some success, but now it is apparent to all. The problem for the Government is that using this measure and using reasonable projections of inflation, employees will be between 10 per cent and 16 per cent worse off over the two years of the Social Contract with the majority of the loss coming in this second year. If anything will mitigate against the smooth running of this phase, this fact alone will do so.

What of the future? As we endure economic crisis after economic crisis, whether it manifests itself as inflation or as a balance of payments problem, it is likely that there will be a further pressure to impose restraints on free collective bargaining. In between times the trade union movement and the membership will attempt to rectify the changes between relative rates of pay resulting from these policies. One thing is abundantly clear. A market economy cannot sustain nationally administered salaries for any length of time. The labour market is a sensitive area and any constraints imposed upon it on the remuneration side leads to bottlenecks and shortages of skilled personnel in economic upswings. In the longer term incomes policy will distort relativities to such an extent as to make some jobs totally unfillable. The probable outcome is that ministerial activists will attempt to impose incomes policies at certain times, especially if the economy is not put onto a sounder basic economic footing. These policies will be of the wider, less specific, £6 limit variety, but will not last for more than a period of eighteen consecutive months. The re-entry to free collective bargaining problems still has to be solved. The anomalies created, the differentials and relativities distorted still have to be cured. Centrally-administered wages policies over a longer period would need a radically different political system from the one which we now operate and one which would probably prove to be most unpalatable to the people of Britain.

Chapter 2

Collective agreements

'Keep honour bright' – Troilus and Cressida

The system

Collective bargaining takes place between employers and trade unions; that is a bald descriptive statement. It is however a structured and stratified system, held together by written and verbal agreements between various unions and management, between unions themselves and often cemented by their history.

The first question to arise is which employer bargains with which unions for what group of employees and on what subjects. If no formal system of agreements existed the entire system would be anarchic, employers negotiating with union x one year, union y the next, or thirty unions each representing ten members in alternate years. The uncertainties and fragmentations that would arise from this system would make collective bargaining totally unworkable in Britain. The Industrial Relations Act had sections on representation and bargaining agents and units, but as most of those only applied to 'registered unions' they were unworked if not unworkable.

This is overcome by managements recognising a union, or sometimes unions, as the bargaining agents for clearly-defined groups of employees. Such recognition may sometimes be the fruit of bitter struggles, or alternatively, the employer may have (graciously or otherwise) bowed to the inevitable. In other instances the union may have had to take the problem to the Advisory, Conciliation and Arbitration Service under Section 11 and this is discussed in chapter eleven.

Procedural agreements in general

The cornerstone of collective bargaining in Britain is the procedure agreement and this chapter is devoted to discussing its various forms.

This is not to say that collective bargaining cannot exist without a formal agreement, the Whitley system gives the lie to this and there are examples of verbal agreements in the private sector which have never been put into written form but are adhered to by both parties out of a mutual respect of each other's strength. Nevertheless the normal and formal method of defining the rights which exist between the two parties is by a procedure agreement.

Agreements vary markedly in their scope and content and type. Some are merely a letter from one side to the other confirming the existence of negotiating rights, others run to detailed handbooks which dot every 'i', cross every 't', define every job and leave nothing to chance. Strangely enough when disputes arise over agreements it is usually the latter type, with its rigid interpretations which is more likely to be the cause merely because the sheer complexities offer only limited interpretations and thus constrain bargaining positions. In general terms however it is preferable to have a 'tight' agreement than a loose one. If there is trouble over a text, do it better next time.

Procedure agreements cannot be seen in isolation from the individual's contract of employment. In many cases clauses of the procedure agreement are inserted into the individual contract of employment and prove to be of vital importance. The bugbear of the 1971 Industrial Relations Act was that of legal enforceability. All agreements whether procedural, grievance, delineating substantive conditions or even the agreed minutes of a joint meeting used to have to include the prophylactic words 'This agreement is binding in honour only and no part of it is intended to be enforceable in law.' The disclaimer was frequently used in union–management agreements as they re-gained the status of agreements prior to the Industrial Relations Act which presumed that all agreements were not legally binding unless they specifically stated that the intention of the signatories was to the contrary. But an individual's contract of employment *is* legally binding and those elements of the procedure agreement which are written into a personal contract equally become legally binding. The result of this is that all new procedure agreements under the 1971 Act were carefully negotiated and the implications of clauses carefully analysed because it became an unfair industrial practice for an organisation of workers knowingly to induce a person to break (or threaten to break) a contract and the organisation could be liable to unlimited damages awarded against it.

This absurdity has now gone but the danger could be guarded against only by the precise wording of the procedure agreement including the notice necessary to promote industrial action or an ingenious 'double disclaimer'. This was widely written into the procedure agreement and stated 'nothing in this agreement shall restrict the right to undertake industrial action by extending the notice required to suspend a contract of employment beyond X (usually seven) days'. This means that a notice to take strike action also stands as a notice to suspend the collective bargaining provisions incorporated in the contract of employment, from the collective agreement.

Free of that, we now come onto the types of procedure agreement being drafted today. There are many categories but the main issue is whether it is national or local although there are many cases where both are in existence. Industry in Britain today does not revolve around the single-plant entrepreneurial employer so beloved of Adam Smith and subsequently the neo-classicist economists and politicians. British Industry is basically oligopolistic with the large, multi-plant, multi-product or service company dominating the scene. The tendency for growth has been on a vertically integrated production pattern; for example a motor manufacturer would buy up an accessory company. This trend has been reversed in recent years and a random integration has been in vogue using the holding company device. This conglomerate company may have many totally different companies, offering totally different services and producing totally disparate products, e.g. ITT, Slater Walker or Thomas Tilling. A third alternative is to have a multi-plant company producing similar if not identical items, i.e., International Computers Ltd. Each of these examples have one thing in common, they all have more than one site for their business operations and the employees as such can then be represented at a site level, a head office or national level or a combination of the two.

National level

A typical National Agreement normally covers all the eligible employees throughout Britain. A clear example of this type of agreement is the one between the Ford Motor Company and ASTMS. The agreement provides for national negotiations held at the Head Office of the Company and conducted between the National Officials of ASTMS and the Industrial Relations department of the company. Individual grievances, the procedure for which is now written into the individual contracts of employment, are dealt with at plant level by the elected representatives in the first instance, the local Officer, if there is no resolution of the problem, and finally by a national official as a last resort. The Ford system thus gives all plants the same negotiating date, the same increases and does not allow for any on-plant negotiations on salaries and conditions of service.

Domestic agreements

A local agreement is diametrically opposite to this and is used in the smaller single plant company or the larger company whose policy is to delegate industrial relations responsibilities down the line. The General Electric Company, a huge employer, is an example of this type of relationship. There is no national negotiating agreement, indeed there is no provision to negotiate on any topic affecting all staff. This can prove to be a handicap when items common to all such as a new pension scheme fails to be negotiated because the procedure to do so does not exist and the subject does not lend itself to piecemeal local efforts. However, there is now a widespread feeling for change on such issues as staff pensions. This is one disadvantage of this type of procedural system when it is rigidly applied. Each GEC plant negotiates at different times with the local management negotiating with first, the employee representatives, and subsequently the local officer. The company claim that there is no mandatory, overall industrial relations or personnel policy and this is carried to extremes when a negotiation on redundancy compensation, a frequent occurrence in GEC, is carried out at local level even though the decision on resources which created the redundancies is patently a centralised one.

Mixed agreements

Most GEC plants are members of the Engineering Employers Federation; some are not. This adds to the overall inchoate appearance of the negotiating machinery. Such a situation is not unique as some British Leyland plants are federated and others are not. In addition to plant agreements and negotiations, it is possible to have Divisional agreements, the Division generally being based on a product group. British Leyland divide the company into product groups each with their own industrial relations departments and agreements; thus Austin Morris will negotiate separately from the Truck and Bus Division although in a real sense these are both national negotiations over a product range.

At the Chrysler Motor Company the procedure agreement allows for the negotiations of wages and conditions to be done at plant level, i.e., Coventry negotiates independently of Linwood in Scotland and both negotiate independently of Hills Plastics and other Chrysler UK owned non-motor car plants. There is however provision in the agreement to negotiate national questions on a national basis, and a new pension scheme was negotiated using this procedure.

Master agreements

A final form of agreement is a generalised procedure agreement with the head office of the company which lays down the criteria on which recognition will be given on a plant by plant or departmental basis. This type of agreement exists mainly in staff areas where unionisation is to some extent new, and avoids constant clashes and friction. Both Rolls-Royce 1971 and Courtaulds are good examples of companies using this form of procedure agreement.

Contents of agreements

Having delineated which basic type of procedure agreement is to be used the question then arises of what goes into it. Will it be a full or partial agreement, will it give only representational rights or full negotiating rights, and what stages are to be written into the agreement? It can be argued that the procedure agreement does more than provide a framework for industrial relations and negotiations; that it actually determines the course the negotiations will take and the eventual outcome. This argument is similar to the one that states whoever writes the agenda of a meeting can control the outcome and decisions of that meeting – a tenable hypothesis.

The first distinction to be made is between representational and negotiating agreements. A representational agreement is one where the management agrees to allow an individual member, or in a collective representational situation all members, to be represented by either a lay- or full-time official of the trade union. Representations are not negotiations, they are more akin to advocacy or consultation. Negotiating implies an equality between the parties both of whom have the same ability to influence the outcome. Representations merely confer the right to be heard but even if all the arguments used are overwhelmingly just there is no commitment to any action, and no constraints can be imposed. The commitment is only to listen. This is most unsatisfactory and can be regarded as a temporary situation, where it exists, and as a 'thin end of the wedge' tactic; it is a classic defence used by the most anti-trade union employers basically in the hope that the organised staffs will suffer a loss of morale because of inadequate material returns.

It has been hoped that this will change under the impact of the Advisory Conciliation and Arbitration Service established under the Employment Protection Act and able to deal with recognition questions from 1 February 1976. The procedure agreement can contain not only the negotiating procedure in a collective bargaining sense but also the grievance procedure on behalf of individual members. It is not unusual for both sets of procedure to be in the same document but this is not necessary; in fact a management can have many agreements with a trade union each covering a different industrial relations aspect. Let us assume that only one agreement exists and that this covers all the points which may arise. The first and singularly important clause is to define the parties to the agreement in the most precise terms; whether the party on the management side is a small company or a parent company of a plant or even a holding company can be crucial.

The next question to be answered is what categories of employees are to be included in the agreement. These must be carefully delineated and described to avoid clashes with other trade unions who may be organising similar categories of employees – the so-called 'grey areas'. It may be, for example, that all technical staffs are subject to the agreement or only technical staffs in certain specified departments. When a new section of employees have been enrolled in the required strength to get recognition either a separate agreement can be signed or this group of employees can be added to the existing list. It is possible to have a procedure agreement which stipulates the conditions and numbers of any group of employees to be covered before recognition is granted, and separate annexes to the agreement signed as these groups attain the negotiated recognition criteria.

Once the parties to the agreement have been adequately identified the contents of the agreement must be negotiated. These can vary widely as stated from a simple statement of the type: 'Negotiations between the parties will be on salaries and conditions of service' to a long and detailed list of negotiated topics, specific to each group of workers, all the stages in each separate negotiation listed; some to thirty or forty sides of print. In addition a grievance procedure is often written into the agreement as a separate section which really makes the document a 'procedure agreement'.

A rough but typical guide to the stages involved in the negotiating side is as follows:

(1) the claim is presented by the lay members in the plant through the representatives or shop stewards; if this does not result in an agreement with the management team then:

(2) the full-time officer of the Union will meet the plant personnel department; if this does not result in an agreement then:

(3) the responsible national officer will meet either the central personnel department or senior managers or directors of the plant; if this does not result in an agreement;

(4) a 'failure to agree' is registered.

Other intermediate steps can be, and sometimes are, inserted and often a time limit is placed on each stage; that is to say between stages two and three a space of three weeks is typically imposed. The time lag is intended to give both sides time for reflection or appreciation of the position, but it can prove a frustrating waiting period and a time when opinions harden. In some agreements there is an extra stage which is generally some form of arbitration and the conditions are set down for the appointment of an arbiter.

A grievance procedure will follow on the same lines except that generally the initial stage is an approach by the aggrieved employee to his immediate or relevant superior followed by an approach to this superior by the group representative (or shop steward). The procedure then follows that laid down for bargaining purposes.

Special clauses

In most procedure agreements there is a clause which states that both the union and management have the long-term interests of the employees and company very much in mind. There are other clauses which can be inserted into an agreement. The two most controversial are the 'status quo' and 'management prerogative' clauses which are the opposite sides of the same coin. The 'status quo' clause deals with changes in works procedure or employment conditions and states that when any such changes are to be made and prior agreement has not been reached the 'status quo' shall prevail whilst negotiations proceed. Not unnaturally this has been a union choice of clause. The 'management prerogative' side is exactly the opposite. It reserves the right for the management to manage and to dispose of changes in employment conditions, etc., without negotiations of any description with the union. This is a management clause, is basically a North American import and was responsible in one celebrated case for a twelve-week, white-collar strike at Henry Wiggin and Company in Hereford in 1973 after which the clause was finally removed.

The subjects covered in procedural agreements are generally wages and conditions of service but they can also cover specific items such as redundancies, early retirements, special overseas allowances, clothes allowances and a host of problems which may be specific to one employer. It is possible to have an agreement covering each distinct item, or to put them together; in practical terms it makes little difference.

Whether or not the procedural agreement itself dictates the shape of the negotiations, or the outcome, is also not significant. But, marginally, if specified stages are laid down in the agreement it is likely that these stages will all be used as there is, as it were, a last resort – the buck can pass. If a 'National Officer stage' is present it is tempting for both sides to take the case to such a stage in the hope that there may be 'something in it for them'. Should an arbitration clause be inserted it is more likely for procedure to reach this stage than if it is exhausted at a National Officer level and there is only industrial action left. Some agreements have been signed by weaker unions where 90 per cent of the text has described the preparations for and the setting up of arbitration machinery. This clause is often an indication not of reasonableness and logic but of the weakness of the trade union or the lack of faith of its leaders in their membership support.

Procedure agreements are interesting in that they are generally adhered to; it was and is unusual for either side to accuse the other of breaking the agreement. One reason for the trade union antagonism to the Industrial Relations Act was its implicit assumption that unions could not be trusted and that legally binding clauses had to prevail. This was flying in the face of all known knowledge on the subject. The Stock Exchange proudly boasts that its transactions are based on honour; a handshake and a deal is clinched. From time to time someone defaults in this system, yet if it were suggested that all transactions were to be written because the honour system was not sufficiently strong there would be a huge outcry.

Joint union panels, employers' federations

A procedure agreement need not be between one union and one employer, it can be between many unions and one employer, many employers and one union, and many employers and many unions. This can get confusing so it is best to deal with these one by one. Unions can form a loose confederation for the purpose of negotiations where either strength or orderly industrial relations indicate this is the best method. The Civil Air Transport industry is a case in point. The staff side of the industry's National Joint Council has a procedure agreement with the employers' side of the industry. There are fourteen signatory unions in the industry, each with clearly demarcated zones of influence and each can conduct its own specific negotiations through the auspices of the NJC. The NJC staff side appoints its own secretary, chairman and guiding committee and these co-ordinate the policies and claims. The employers' side, which represents the major airlines, has a similar arrangement and a permanent secretariat in London. The result has been a degree of co-ordination between both the unions and airlines on their respective sides to the benefit of the growth of the industry and a service to the public.

The Confederation of Shipbuilding and Engineering Unions is a formal confederation of trade unions with its own secretariat. It not only acts as a useful meeting forum for unions with members within its industries but it holds, in its own right, procedure agreements with the Engineering Employers' Association for manual workers and with the Shipbuilding Employers for a wider group. This is the first time we have analysed the concept of an employers' association and it is fitting that its first mention should be of the most powerful, though in many of their policies, the most backward of them all.

There are many employers' associations in Britain (1,135 as compared with 109 TUC-affiliated unions) and they act as trades unions of employers, not for employees, in the same way as a normal trade union operates. Employers' associations could have been registered under the Industrial Relations Act but even the Registrar had great difficulty in explaining the advantages of registration to their officials and members. An employers' association draws its membership from the companies within its industry. The larger employer associations such as the Engineering Employers control the bargaining arrangements within the industry by insisting that only unions that are recognised by the Association can negotiate with its member companies. The Engineering Employers have a stratified and highly organised federation to conduct their relationships with the trade unions at local and national levels. The Federation is split into various District Associations each of which can conduct negotiations and advise their local members. There is a large central secretariat which negotiates, runs an advisory service and acts as a policy making body for the Federation. If one member suffers a strike a contingency fund subscribed to by other members may tide them over losses of revenue.

Member firms of the Engineering Employers' Federation will only negotiate with trade unions which have an agreement with the Federation. It is not necessary for a company to federate all of its plants or subsidiaries; as already indicated some companies have a mixture of federated and non-federated subsidiaries or plants. Conditions between these various sectors often show marked disparities in negotiated conditions and in the negotiating method and this represents a rather unsatisfactory arrangement. On the other hand, a strong, opportunistic union can happily leapfrog in these situations.

A union's agreement with the Federation is in a sense akin to enabling legislation. It provides that where a union has membership in certain specified areas the member companies will afford recognition to the union. It is a far more civilised method of gaining recognition than the industrial strife and bitterness that can accompany a recognition problem. The company or plant sometimes signs a procedure agreement on behalf of the appropriate groups or employees with the union and bargaining then takes place. Sometimes they do not. One can get a situation where two procedure agreements exist, one a federated agreement using their procedure and facilities and the other a normal one-off type of agreement laying down procedures to be followed. In these cases it is normal for the domestic agreement to take precedence over the federation one; fortunately there are few anarchists in permanent industrial relations posts and few procedurally impossible situations.

The negotiating procedures within the Engineering Employers' Federation are quite complex and moreover vary from union to union. The agreements are basically concerned with two elements: the formal negotiating procedure and the delineation of members to be recognised for bargaining purposes. The old ASTMS agreements show up this system in stark relief. Because ASTMS was formed as an amalgamation of two unions, ASSET and AScW, both of which had individual agreements the new body had two procedure agreements, Division 1 and Division A which, although similar, had slight bargaining differences but obviously major differences in recruitment areas.

In bargaining terms the procedure was roughly as follows. Attempts were made to settle the claims at a domestic level using both in-plant and local conferences. The local conference is based on the full-time union officer and his negotiating counterpart from the Federation meeting at the local Engineering Employers offices, along with union members and representatives of the company involved. If a settlement was not reached the case would then be transferred to Central Conference in London where a union official and a national level EEF employee would try to settle the issue. For there to be industrial action of any description within the terms of the agreement this stage of procedure had to be exhausted yet on average it took four months for a claim to reach national level after it had been originally submitted. Given this long time-lag either indifference or militancy is reinforced amongst the union membership, but in either event only the most severe of injustices provoked disputes. At one stage ASTMS were processing almost twenty national level cases per week which was an intolerable level given the low settlement rate.

Although the procedure agreements remain extant there is now an informal agreement between the EEF and the union. This is to virtually ignore the final, national-level stage unless either side insist, and providing both agree procedure is exhausted after the Local Conference stage. The number of cases now reaching London is down to about five a month. Naturally this has simplified administration for both sides without noticeably affecting either the dispute record or the settlement record.

Recognition

The recognition question is separate from this. In the white-collar union sector the EEF have agreements with five trade unions. In the past there has been a rigid demarcation of eligible grades, that is to say that a member company of the EEF would only afford recognition to a union if it had members and were in one of the groups specified in the centrally-held agreement. Although this was fine in theory, in practice employers, under pressure, tended to recognise unions if they had a substantial membership in areas outside of the master agreement. This situation arises particularly where unions, although they hold the master agreement have recruited no members in certain companies, not because there is any resistance to unionisation but because the union concerned lacked either sufficient resources or energies. Equally there are always 'grey areas' where job titles overlap or new technologies create new jobs not covered by existing agreements.

This *ad hoc* agreement has now been formalised. In future where a union is not entitled to recognition under a National Agreement but has 'a significant presence' and is a 'major influence' in the grade, recognition will be, dependent on the local employer's attitude of course, granted. The TUC dispute principles and existing bargaining arrangements take precedence, not unnaturally, over this new development. It should lead to a higher overall level of unionisation in the white-collar sector of the engineering industry. For the most part the national agreement specifies recognition for substantial membership or other loosely defined criteria.

Outside of such master agreements recognition is somewhat more haphazard. Naturally the union must have some membership in the areas where it is seeking recognition although this does not always follow. An employer may well wish to have no unions for his workers, but given a choice will try to arrange for the least effective and potentially more amenable union to obtain negotiating rights. It is not unknown in British industry for a trade union to be 'given' negotiating rights for a group of employees where they have no members at all, merely as a pre-emptive ploy by the management. The result is known as a 'sweetheart agreement'.

There is a critical point in trying to get recognition with a company because of the peculiar position a trade union is in. An employee joins a union and his subscription pays that union for services which it can provide, but, until a sufficient number of people join the services are not available. It becomes a sophisticated exercise to persuade the last few members to join in order to provide recognition for the whole. Some companies like ICI realised this and refused staff union recognition and indeed went to extraordinary lengths to prevent it and as a result the ASTMS membership in ICI grew in certain areas, dwindled when recognition did not come, rose in other areas and subsequently fell and a whole cycle of new membership and lapsing built up. This is now over in most ICI areas and the company is revising its attitudes although painfully and still with prejudice. But even the National Industrial Relations Court found that ICI were not abiding by the Code of Practice. The old pre-Industrial Relations Act's Commission of Industrial Relations were well aware of this vicious-circle problem and instead of auditing membership pioneered the attitude survey with questions such as 'if "X" union were granted recognition would you join?' This is a far more reliable indicator of employees' feelings on union membership than a plain head count, and is valid where there has been a hostile employer who had been opposing union membership and representation.

In the normal run of events the local officer will approach the company in writing asking for recognition when the officer feels that there are sufficient members to make this a viable proposition. In a one-off company situation the solution has been straightforward; either 'yes' and a procedure agreement is signed, or 'no' and then either industrial action is called for and taken or the officer goes back to recruiting and presents his claim for recognition at a later date. This has been the pattern until the Employment Protection Act. Now a union can complain legally to the Advisory Conciliation and Arbitration Service.

The multi-plant company is a totally different proposition. It is possible for a large multi-plant concern to thwart recognition by using the structure of the work-force. The difficulty in recruiting the marginal members for recognition to be granted has been out-lined. A multi-plant company can compound this by insisting on ballots of the membership across different product groups and large geographical distances, or by grade splitting or amalgamating constituencies; in short gerrymandering. The company may insist on national agreements only and forcing a ballot on a country-wide basis; it can also insist that this ballot does not succeed if 50 per cent + 1 vote for the union overall, rather this majority has to be reached at each individual plant, although the agreement will be national. These ploys have been tried in the past and to some extent succeeded for a decade especially in the petro-chemical industry. Fortunately, logical argument backed by the industrial strength that increased membership brings is ending this sort of chicanery. A ballot of the members in question still remains the favourite criterion of recognition in some industries although the percentage required varies as does the type of recognition – national or local. Again the use of the Advisory, Conciliation and Arbitration Service reference will modify this. Once recognition has been granted and a formal agreement signed union recruitment increases dramatically, but can only be maintained if the union services the members in a thoroughly professional way and delivers what it promises.

Bridlington procedure

Poaching of one union's members by another used to lead to industrial disputes and pressure for rigid demarcation lines. The TUC 'Bridlington and Croydon procedures' for the avoidance of disputes have now removed this as a major source of friction. It is these agreements that prevent a trade union recruiting members of another union. All TUC-affiliated unions are bound by the Bridlington procedures which normally provide for transfer of membership only if the union whose member wishes to leave, agrees to the transfer. If a dispute arises the TUC may set up a tribunal known as a Disputes Committee and although its decision is binding in honour only it is invariably adhered to – or, to quantify, has only seriously been challenged twice since the Second World War. Unions make representations at these meetings and sometimes important points of principle are at stake. This system provides the stability of membership which the procedural agreement system needs to function smoothly.

If this system provides the framework for orderly industrial relations, it is only a framework. It is based on an honour system, both parties realising they have much to lose if they break procedure. The history is chequered; thousands of men and women in Britain lost their jobs or were black-listed because they had the temerity to try to organise a union organisation within their company. Many disputes followed from these victimisations and from intransigent employers refusing perfectly reasonable requests for recognition. But, once won, the job for the union has only just started. The next step is to negotiate on behalf of these members and to represent their interests in all facets of their working lives by all the means available, both traditional and unorthodox. The rest of this short book is devoted to explaining how this is done in a complex, modern, industrial society but with the Employment Protection legislation now providing an armoury of weapons for the ways and the means.

Chapter 3

National claims

'Avarice. the spur of industry' – Hume

Work and salary

Hume, the great Scots philosopher and economist was a true product
of his time and upbringing; imbued with the Protestant ethic and a
classical economist his slogan 'Avarice the Spur of Industry' was to
him not a condemnation but a justification of the system. Or, for
the majority, how is one to get money if not to work for it? One can
of course be born into enough money to preclude being industrious
but the British distribution of wealth is such that you have more
chance of being killed by a falling chimney stack. If you are one of
the wage earners or salariat of this world you will know that working
harder will not necessarily bring more money, but one thing is
certain; salaries and wages are a compensation for entering the
labour market, for the time spent doing something which is all too
often disagreeable or boring.

The society in which we live is based on money and expectations
of money, and these are seen as the signs of success. It need not be so,
for some societies have substituted honours or status in lieu of
money and in Britain the patronage system allegedly used to be
enough to keep subpostmistresses and senior civil servants hard at it
year in year out. The basic motivation, however, is money and the
goods and services it buys are the chief incentive. In recent years
employees have shown a tendency to trade-off money against
improvements in hours and conditions of work. The expectations of
money are as important as its actual acquisition, advertising reinforces the general ethos of escalating expectations, the colour
television has replaced the black and white, the stereo record player
replaces the standard, cars must be changed more regularly, fashions
change more quickly, but advertising doesn't provide the money to
finance these symbols of success.

A wage or salary is the end product of a bargaining process and a bargain struck between the employer and the employee and that bargain can be made by an individual or on a collective basis by a trade union acting as the agent. There are ten million trade union members in Britain and nearly all of these have their pay determined by the collective bargaining mechanism. In addition, there are a probable one million whose salaries are fixed by reference to wages boards and central mechanisms but who are not members of trade unions and yet a further four million whose salaries are effectively fixed by negotiations between a union and employer but who are not union members. This latter section is often quite anti-trade union, deploring its militancy yet always accepting the fruits of that militancy and expertise; they have been described by union members as malcontent freeloaders.

The collective bargaining process is at the heart of trade union activity but although the most publicised probably only accounts for 50 per cent of all time of the full-time officials in a modern, general-type union. It is also the process that affects the greatest percentage of members at any one time and the one that is the most important to their well-being. As a general rule it is not sufficient for a trade union simply to seek to maintain the real living standards of its membership; it must try to improve those standards as well as the in-work environmental conditions and all relevant conditions of service. This aim can only be achieved by regular, steady increases in disposable income over and above the concurrent increases in the cost of living. If the union is content to maintain real purchasing power it argues that it and its members are all satisfied with their station in life. One misconception that must be removed at this stage is that an increase for those not on the bottom rungs of an industry must be at the expense of the lower-paid or in elementary and abused jargon of government ministers the 'National Cake' consists only of salaries and wages. This is patently untrue. Increases can be financed out of profits, out of increases in productivity or general taxation revenue which should be (but sadly is not) based on a progressive system. Incomes must not be confused with wealth and what is required is to redistribute some of that wealth in the form of incomes rather than having one group of workers played off against the other.

As we have seen in the preceding chapter the procedure agreement lays down the framework and ground rules of the negotiations and there are basically two main types – national negotiations and local negotiations. This chapter is devoted to the national negotiation, the different types, the preparation of the claim, the procedures and the settlements and how they applied: chapter four is devoted to the local negotiations which usually embrace different considerations.

Type of national negotiation

National negotiations can be held in the following circumstances but dependent on the form of procedure agreement. There are situations where all salariat package bargaining starts and finishes at national level, e.g., the Ford Company, the Prudential Assurance Company, the National Coal Board or British Airways. Alternatively there are national negotiations where the procedure at local levels has to be exhausted and the negotiation processed through to national level. There is also bargaining undertaken under the auspices of an agreement with an Employers Federation where the claim has been processed from a local employers' Association to a National Federation. The latter case is one which typically can give rise to the negotiation of basic minima nationally followed by local negotiations then fixing the actual remuneration. National negotiations also differ in that they may establish the wages and conditions across an entire industry, for example the Post Office, may establish wages and conditions across all plants of a multi-plant company, for example, Fords, or may establish wages and conditions at one small company or one plant of a multi-plant company. In short, agreed national-level negotiating procedures cover a wide spectrum and are used for differing purposes dependent upon the terms of the agreement under which the negotiations are held.

National officials

Trade unions are notable for their difference in internal organisation' terms of service and powers of full-time officials, shop stewards' representatives; different job titles for similar jobs all divide union from union. Yet there is one job description in common, no matter the designation and that is the officer with national responsibilities. But in private industry and commerce most trade unions will also have officers (full-time officials) who are responsible for an area, a region or a division and these officers will deal with negotiations, recruitment and general industrial problems in their area of responsibility. Typically, the hierarchy is defined on a geographical responsibility basis so that those officials with national responsibilities will be senior to those with more closely defined local duties. It is on this hierarchial nature that the national negotiation depends, and why it is inserted at such a late stage in some procedure agreements. The assumption is that although local officials may have to refer offers or wait for decisions from the national officials, thus slowing negotiations, the national officials are capable of taking these decisions in negotiations, after consultations with the membership. Thus, obvious as it may sound, national negotiations have just one factor in common, they are conducted, on the trade union side by national officers. If nothing else, managements must then observe strict protocol and always have their side represented by managers of senior grade with, if appropriate to the company, national responsibilities too. Briefly, they must have the power to settle or move decisively towards a settlement.

It is the national negotiation which generally hits the industrial relations headlines and it is the national officer who becomes the trade union spokesman. When asked about strikes most people will recall various public service actions, railwaymen, dustmen, electricity workers, airline pilots or miners, all stemming from national negotiations and the only time a local dispute will be mentioned is in general terms (say) about the motor car industry. It is not the method of negotiations which is known; it is the break-down of negotiations.

The period of agreements

The time interval between one set of national negotiations and the next varies as to which type of negotiations are to be undertaken and also the provisions of the previous negotiations. The 'national only' negotiation recurrence depends on the settlement at the last round, usually this is now of one year's duration; they have been spread over two or three years although this has become rare in periods of inflation. The habit of a year-plus settlement is an import from North America and American-based 'British' companies are its main advocates. In a way it is similar to buying futures in the stock market, the longer the period the greater the uncertainty and risk but the greater the possible returns.

A two-year agreement can be generous in its provisions but the gamble the trade union takes is that prevailing economic conditions, distorted by inflation and government monetary and fiscal policies, are not more disadvantageous to the members in the second year than the agreement potentially compensates for. Thus negotiations can be annual, biennial or triennial: there have been none longer. In the intervening period the agreement generally stipulates that there will be no further claims of a central economic nature. This does not preclude negotiations to change a procedure agreement for example or on job restructuring, redundancies or individual grievances.

The only description that one can make of the time periods between national negotiations in other instances is that there are no fixed intervals although occasionally a pattern emerges because of comparisons with other groups. Because the negotiations only go into the final stages when the previous stages have failed to yield a settlement the interval between collective bargaining taking place and national negotiations need not be the same. It may be that in year one a settlement was reached at national level, at year two building on this previous settlement all bargaining was completed at local level and in year three it was back to national level; alternatively all agreements may have been completed at local level. The pattern once established is not easily broken and once a case has been taken to national level an employer will not concede a halfpenny until the final stages, and a union cannot generally take local industrial action before this stage is reached as it would be in breach of procedure. This situation obtains most often with companies who are members of an Employers' Federation.

It is possible to have a settlement which allows the trade union side the chance to re-open negotiations before the next due date, for example after six months when the settlement is to run for one year. This is especially valuable in times of government interference in the collective bargaining process which constrains increases but which may be lifted or amended at a future date, a date which can vary due to prevailing short-term economic effects. Inflation makes it an equally valuable device especially when there is no threshold or other automatic cost-of-living compensation device in operation; its usefulness in this case is that employees do not have to wait a full year to re-establish their real purchasing power as negotiated in the last settlement. In this respect, ideally, a negotiated settlement will impute an inflation rate for the life of the settlement and this should be added onto the increase. If it is on the low side it is made up at the next negotiation, if on the higher side it is deducted from the following year's estimate: this gives the employee cover against inflation at or before it happens which is a far more satisfactory state of affairs than always being behind.

Remuneration v. wages

All negotiations in the 'wage round' are about money in the end but not nowadays necessarily an increase in salary; indeed this may be by far the worst option for the employee. If a man or woman is paying tax at standard rate every pound increase negotiated is, in disposable terms, only 65 pence. If, on the other hand, the one pound increase is taken in terms of other elements in the salariat package which the employee would otherwise have to purchase out of his or her 65 pence the employee is incontestably better off to the tune of 35 pence. In terms of a £350 a year increase this is a net gain of £122.50 if it is all taken in elements other than money. Although the Truck Acts* do not apply to staff employees it would now seem that their repeal would benefit some other employees. The other elements in the package are diverse but can include company cars, car mileage allowances and car depreciation allowances, concessionary mortgage rates and insurance rates, housing subsidies or company houses, improved pension arrangements, travel concessions or vouchers, indeed vouchers of all descriptions and these are only the tip of the iceberg. When negotiations are held, some form of case to justify the increases should be made and this requires some amplification. It really cannot safely be asserted that the success of collective bargaining, whether local or national, is directly correlated to the justness, sophistication or even the detailed basis of the claim. There is however no doubt that there is *some* correlation although the reasons for this are not as apparent as one would think or like to believe.

The claim

A management is sensitive to charges of exploitation or parsimony and if a well-argued and researched case is publicly aired it can prove a great source of embarrassment. Some employers are actually convinced by such a case and take the appropriate actions and it is noticeable how many employers will now argue the points raised in the claim, some going to the extent of publishing counter arguments. One of the most important effects of a good claim however is on the membership of the union. A well-thought-out claim should explain to the membership exactly why the demands are as presented, and as such has an educative function as well as often instilling some militancy. People are sensible, they will not take industrial action and lose money, or in extreme cases jeopardise promotion prospects or even their jobs, unless they are convinced that this is the only way they can achieve their objectives and it is vital they are also seized of the justice of their case. In present circumstances every man and woman in Britain can see the increase in prices of food, petrol, fares, clothing and other essentials but what is needed is to inform the members how much their money has depreciated, what the profits of their employers are, what others are earning and so on. With this

---

* These were Acts of Parliament which outlawed the payment of workers in kind or by goods from company-owned shops.

in mind there is obviously no point in producing a highly sophisticated claim, full of economic and business terminology, which makes
an exposition of marginal theory, shadow pricing and explains all
about non-linear programming because few of the members will
understand it. It is not an academic exercise. There have been very
sophisticated national claims, which were not conspicuously
successful, one reason being they were not prepared by the union's
own research department and their comprehensibility to the average
member was of a low order. A different style was adopted by
ASTMS on behalf of members at the Pearl Assurance Company by a
combination of members and the research department. Hopefully
it has learned from others' mistakes. It was readily comprehensible;
the graphs when used were simple and easy to read, all data had been
converted to index form and the accounts had been minutely
examined but with simple explanations. It may be that in this
liaison lies the most productive method of drawing up formal claims.

The content of the claims varies as much as their depth and
depends on whether the employer is in the private or public sector,
whether it is a one-off plant or part of a multi-plant enterprise,
indeed a multi-national company. There are, however, key essentials
that must be included. The rate of inflation since the last settlement,
or over the last three years, must both be set against the increases
negotiated in the periods. The food index is similarly correlated
especially if there are any groups of lower-paid employees involved
in the claim. Salaries of employees with similar job descriptions (not
titles) working in other concerns in the same industry or in different
industries or in the public sector are taken into account plus the
internal differentials within the enterprise and how they have
changed since the last settlement or longer period.* All these points
can be made as appropriate and must be accurate, there is nothing
worse than giving an employer a stick with which to beat the
employees' representative's case. In the case of comparative salaries
only higher salaries are normally documented and unless the
company is the industry leader this can be productive. If this appears
biased the management will always redress the balance by quoting
only lower salaries. Finally, apart from specific company or industry
details and prospects (including EEC membership effects) there is
the question of profitability and productivity. This is a most vexed
and vexing question and must be dealt with in more detail.

---

* In the unusual retail price index volatility of 1974–6 it has also become
essential for union bargainers to be able to make a very measured estimate
of the future trends in order to assemble a suitable mixture of tactics to
protect purchasing power while assessing job content, productivity and value.

The definition of profits is itself unclear; in a nice unlittered and simplistic world it would be the excess of income over expenditure in any given accounting period. But what is income, what is expenditure? What about taxation, investment grants and depreciation methods? There may be many accounts consolidated into one account, special funds may be set up, profits may or may not be distributed. In a multi-plant, multi-company situation such as Unilever with separate 'free-standing' companies, does one look at the main accounts or the subsidiaries' accounts, has there been transfer pricing? In a multi-national company there are these problems plus international transfers of capital for tax reasons and transfers of plant and components and other assets to and from overseas companies. The negotiator's problems are immense. The published company accounts are the only widely available source of information on this subject but are not sufficiently detailed to make the sort of analysis which is needed. Accounts are generally produced to reassure or attract shareholders and not to give an overall, financial picture of the company so basically the average shareholder is no better off than a trade union in that the information provided is still very limited. Rolls-Royce was the classic example of the unreliability of company accounts. Reading the accounts prior to 1971 it appeared that they were making modest profits but what in fact was happening was that development costs, instead of being added to the debit side of the account, were treated as an increase in capital and, incidentally, new share issues seem to have been floated on what was essentially a loss.

Given the problems, until company law is changed to provide fuller accounts and accounting procedures standardised and the law provides for full disclosure to employees, unions must make do with the published material. It must be scrutinised thoroughly to see if assets are being hidden or profits understated. Any statistics which are to be used such as profit per head of employee, capital per head of employee, return on capital, etc., are easily worked out (except that capital is as difficult as profits to grasp) and presented in readable form. Some accounts such as those of a large insurance company can be exceptionally difficult to understand and follow. It is essential to take all profits both distributed and retained and also to use a run of at least three years, to show the trends in profits, productivity and employment. This still leaves the problems of multi-plant and multi-national companies. As a general rule the parent company should be looked at. The British Leyland Motor Company could have been making a loss on one division but a profit overall or vice versa but British Leyland Motor Company were the employers and the company quoted on the Stock Exchange;

investors could not get a return on Jaguar or Triumph cars or Land Rovers alone: occasionally the reverse is true but this will depend on the internal mechanisms of the company; some companies insist on each subsidiary being self-sufficient – its own profit centre – especially in a conglomerate. Multi-nationals pose a problem that has not yet been solved and this is dealt with in more detail in chapter ten.

The negotiating process

Having worked out the claim, what does the national official do with it? In the case of negotiations which start and finish at national level it is presented to the company at a formal meeting between the union and management – the first procedural stage. This meeting and presentation of the claim comes well before the due date of settlement, for example, if an agreement is to terminate in June the first meeting may take place in April. This allows for time to be used by both sides to reframe claims or often to consult members on the one hand, boards of directors or management committees on the other, and still have the new settlement ready for the time the old one expires. Should the negotiations drag on or be late for some reason there is little problem in that the increases can always be backdated to the end of the last settlement (unless an inter-ventionist government imposes arbitrary settlement dates). Some officials read out the entire claim, word for word, others precis it and add their own comments and this can take some considerable time. The line-up on either side typically is that the union have a National Official leading and probably a research assistant along with three or four representatives of the union committee, these representing different sites when appropriate, the employer's side will comprise of the head of Industrial Relations and three or four other managers generally at least two of whom represent peripheral sites. The management then physically receive the written claim.

In exceptional circumstances, when there is an adjournment (either side can ask for an adjournment), the management side return with an offer, which is then considered in an adjournment by the union side and they may accept or reject the offer. In more usual circumstances the management take the claim away and return in two or three weeks with an offer and the procedure repeated and it may take several such meetings before a settlement is reached.

In British manufacturing industry it is unusual to find a company with single union representation, except for white-collar grouping (say) in petrochemicals or food; they are almost all multi-union situations. Where this occurs the procedure is slightly different. Each union on the joint bargaining panel is represented by national officials, one of whom, generally the most senior, or belonging to the largest group, is chairman and deputed to present the claim. Each group of employees represented by the different unions may have dissimilar problems, e.g. one group may work a forty-hour week, another group thirty-seven-and-a-half hours, one group may have overtime payments, another may not. Providing there is a common grading structure covering all of the members in all of the unions there should be no problem. The main claim embraces the basic payment for all, the salary levels for each grade, holiday entitlements, sick-pay entitlements, etc. The individual union problems are then settled at a secondary set of national negotiations, each of which take place between the management and the one union, these negotiations taking the main claim settlement as given and unchangeable. This sort of negotiation is applicable either in a company like Ford or in an entire industry viz. British Rail with the National Union of Railwaymen and Associated Society of Locomotive Engineers and Firemen and Transport Salaried Staffs' Association sealing their different priorities.

Finally either a settlement is reached or a 'failure to agree' is registered. When a settlement is in the offing it can be ratified in several ways and through several procedures which reflect the attitudes and participation of the membership concerned. In any multi-plant company which has a centralised negotiating system the union must arrange for the members in subsidiaries or plants to meet to discuss the formulation of the claim and to monitor or ratify the negotiations. The method by which this is often done is to arrange for permanent Combine Committees, Industry Committees or National Advisory Committees. These have a full-time official as secretary and a lay member (usually from the union National Executive) as chairman and meet as and when necessary. Each plant or subsidiary sends members to the committee and it is generally this body which decides on the objectives in each year's claim. The members who accompany the national official into the negotiations are elected from the members of the larger committee and they report back to the main committee on the details and progress of the bargaining. On occasions the sub-committee of the national committee is empowered to decide whether or not a settlement is satisfactory, in other circumstances it is the entire national committee who take this decision: or finally the committee will only recommend a decision to each site, a vote is taken at each site mandating the delegates and the committee reconvene to ratify or reject the result of the negotiations.

This is the 'official' apparatus: it is sometimes paralleled by a competitive 'unofficial' shop-stewards' organisation. Although sensible unions seek to avoid this competitive situation by making sure the machinery is democratic.

If accepted, the settlement is written out and signed by the company and the national officials of the union thus transforming it into an agreement.

Failure to agree and industrial action

If rejected, a 'failure to agree' is registered and generally this gives little alternative other than for the union members to take a form of industrial action or resort in some industries to establish arbitration machinery. Action is a last resort and, as explained earlier, not something that is lightly undertaken. It can come in various shapes and sizes varying from an all-out strike to guerilla strikes using small groups of workers, overtime ban, work to rules, non-co-operation with management, and tactics such as 'blacking' all foreign-made components. The objective is quite simply to get management back to the negotiating table and make a further offer whilst demonstrating the support of the membership to both management and to the membership themselves. Employers have power. They hire and fire, they control investment decisions which ultimately determine the size and structure of the labour force which together, in our society, is the power to determine the lifestyles and the mental and physical well-being of all employees and their families. No one, not even the most retrogressive of our politicians has suggested that the right to strike or take industrial action should be abolished, for in Britain it is a right painfully won over many years. Yet when industrial action takes place it is often condemned as anti-social even by those who recognise its necessity as a countervailing force against the employer.

In a negotiation the employer generally pleads poverty or that profits are necessary to guarantee steady investment; what the management do not generally explain is the growing inequality in wealth and income distributions and that despite record profits there has not been a satisfactory investment level in Britain. Union research on the profit level of a company often counters the poverty argument but then the negotiators need a constraint to balance that lack of investment (which is a polite way of saying redundancies) and this can only be the threat of some form of industrial action. Several points have to be made about such action. The first is that contrary to some ill-informed opinion, generally expressed by those whose knowledge of trade unionism is inadequate, action is only undertaken after the members involved in a dispute situation have voted to take action. The alternative argument that employees can be intimidated into striking, or are gullible, is to deny the basic premise behind democratic systems, which is that each individual's vote carries equal weight and is cast after mature consideration.

Industrial action is not necessary in the great majority of cases. What is essential is that the employer thinks there will be or that there is a high probability of, such action and this estimate is often sufficient. In classic terms all employers will try to minimise their wage bill by various tactics and the thought in their minds that there might be industrial action gives them a trade-off dilemma of increasing the offer (whatever it might be) against the possibility of disruption of the work that is undertaken. Management resistance depends on several factors. The first is how seriously the threat is taken or, in other words, whether the managers believe it either to be an out-and-out bluff or that even if it is not they calculate that the action will not last long because the union members will not support it. The second point is the vulnerability of the concern at that precise moment in time. In a private manufacturing concern a management may almost welcome a strike at times if, say, the product may not be selling due to the prevailing economic conditions, e.g., cars in a credit squeeze, with each shift only adding to the stockpile whilst a strike saves the company paying salaries for some of this period apart from running down the stockpile. On the other hand a company with high order levels, production bottlenecks, contracts with penalty clauses or new production lines to be launched is more vulnerable and this becomes a high profile rather than low profile case. Many workers (over 50 per cent of all employees now) work in areas where there is no visible physical end product, either in the service industries or for local and central government or their agencies. Any disruption cannot offset profits directly, although a postal workers' or miners' strike can affect profits indirectly, and thus the pressures on the employer are somewhat different. These are the actions where the public become more involved in that refuse is not collected or hospital services are cut and power cuts hit the individual household as well as industry. The pressure is then on the government, whether to subject the population to inconvenience and conceivable danger, as well as create industrial problems, or settle with the union concerned before such action is taken. In the past certain groups of workers have been notably non-militant, for example, hospital workers, electrical power engineers, teachers, firemen or crown civil servants and it is no coincidence that these sections of the workforce became amongst the lowest paid in Britain in relation to their contribution. However, the last few years have shown gross government miscalculation in that all these sections have taken industrial action – not all have won all their points by any means, but at the next claim the government cannot discount the possibility of further action and this will almost certainly be reflected in either the settlement or statutory advantages such as the ones designed to placate the civil service in the Heath government's phases of income freezing.

Certain groups of workers are internally 'high profile' ones in that their importance to the smooth running of the organisation concerned is out of all proportion to their numerical strength whilst others are 'low profile' and exhibit exactly the opposite characteristic. Most computer personnel in a commercial or industrial concern represent a high-profile case because the computer has replaced other personnel or even entire departments and actions on their part can halt invoicing, billing, accounting, salary payments, stock control and in some cases production itself. In macro-economic terms miners constitute a high profile group whilst the civil service is low profile. One characteristic is that actions taken in a high-profile situation tend to be shorter and the employees better paid than those in a low-profile group, which in some senses is justifiable for if a group of employees are that vital to the enterprise this should be reflected in their remuneration. Those employed in direct production areas or direct service areas tend to be in higher-profile situations than those with either back-up indirect responsibilities like drawing offices, research and development departments, etc. When an employer is faced with the possibility of action his calculations include the probable effects of the action and these will depend to a larger extent on the profile of the group of employees in question and one sees far more actions of the low type because employers reason that the union members will not stay out for the length of time necessary for an impact to be made. The status of a group can change dramatically along with management reaction to them. An excellent example of this was the test engineers at Jaguar where they struck at a time when the XJ12 was behind schedule and there were technical problems to be overcome. The management, relieved of the obligation to pay them allowed the strike to run for six weeks but as the engineering problems were ironed out strenuous efforts were made to reach a settlement. The group had moved from a low- to high-profile situation because of the change in external circumstances.

What is the cost of an industrial action? To a union it is the payment of strike pay providing the action is 'official', that is, backed by the body in the union which is charged with the task of endorsing industrial action, with dispute pay varying from union to union. To an employer in the public sector the cost is virtually zero, in fact there may be a net surplus in that the salary bill will be lower for the year, but equally the social costs may be high. Unfortunately we do not have methods of computing social cost and profit in an industrial relations sense so that one can legitimately allocate a zero cost. For an employer in the private sector the cost can be difficult to compute. One reads headlines of '£4,000,000 lost in Motor Industry Strike' but this is not so. In the period of the strike x vehicles are not produced, stockpiles exist, so no sales are lost, and in that time £y is saved on a salary bill and £z on variable cost overheads thus in money terms the cost is £4,000,000 − £$(y + z)$. In addition the shortfall in vehicles (assuming each and every one can be sold) is generally made up within the next quarter and thus the cost is merely that of some increased overtime payment for three months minus £$(y + z)$. This could well mean a net operating profit to the company and the main loss (if any) one of goodwill to customers which if, as in the case of an intermediate industry, is often irrelevant due to industrial concentration, is not significant and in any event is not immediately quantifiable.

What action should be taken? A national context is very different to a local one when discussing industrial action except where the national case is really one based on a local situation which has escalated to national level. Nationally it is more difficult to guarantee a concerted response except in such industries as mining or the docks where, in both cases, the community is generally based on the industry and thus union solidarity is reinforced by social coherence and identities. There is nothing more demoralising than calling for an action which is subsequently unsuccessful; indeed the unions with the best reputations amongst employees are those who, in the short run, get the best returns for employees commensurate with the minimum of dislocation to the members' lives, for an unsuccessful action can set a union's members back for years, especially in a national sense. A strike costs money, a strike by one group of members (high profile) costs less, escalating or random striking can be less expensive for both the union and its members, but each member on strike and his family must make sacrifices. Expense is one factor, effectiveness the other. In an organisation dependent on overtime for its efficient running an overtime ban is as effective, albeit after a longer time lag, as an all-out strike, and the same can apply to sticking to a work rule book (as airline engineers and railwaymen have shown) or non-co-operation with management. The final decision is in the hands of the members although in a national sense only the full-time national official in charge has a complete knowledge of all the differing circumstances and attitudes around the country and can therefore advise the national committee on the courses of action available and the one of choice. The choice will, of course, depend on the importance of the claim, the attitude of the members, the business prospects, the general economic prospects prevailing and the chances of success.

When official industrial action is mooted notice then has to be given to the employer. This notice must correspond to the period of notice in the individual employee's contract of employment, a period varying between one week and one month in practical terms. If the management makes a new offer which is accepted in this period the action is naturally not proceeded with – the ideal situation for all concerned. The larger companies, with established industrial-relations departments, did not rush to the National Industrial Relations Court if insufficient notice was given, mainly because they realised that to do so would break down lines of communication and relationships painstakingly built up over the years. But the smaller companies felt it was better to be safe than poorer – if this was practicable.

National level negotiations

The type of national negotiations which is not of a general national basis but is the result of a procedure agreement in a single plant of a large company or a small employer is a different matter. By the time the national official is involved the claim will have been through a minimum of two stages and both sides' attitudes will be known to a greater degree. Generally a sophisticated case presentation is not necessary, the case presented by the national official is that based on the previous stages generally re-interpreted or with the emphasis changed. The theory behind a case proceeding to national level on this basis is that both the national official on the union side and the senior management representative are more experienced and have more authority to accept, reject, or demand changes in a claim or offer, and are not personally committed to the exchange made at the earlier stages. By and large this is true, probably more so on the management side, for it is this side which is being asked to give either money in one form or other or recognition and the more senior the executive the more discretion he has.

Many disputes have escalated beyond normal expectations because the management had not the authority to settle and the union side saw this as intransigence, because local management dared not admit a lack of authority and lose face. However, the main practical benefit is that at a local level both sides may be represented by officials whose personal prestige is bound up with the progress of the claim and relatively uninvolved personnel brought in from outside the plant may have a greater chance of resolving differences.

In some senses a national case of this type is merely a local claim conducted by national officials with all the intense parochial feeling and pressures. Bargaining takes place as in a normal, local claim but in this case the choice of whether to apply sanctions is a little easier in that only one group of workers need be consulted, it is not necessary to convene meetings of a committee drawn from all parts of the United Kingdom (this delays matters) and strength of feeling can be more accurately gauged by both the union and management. Given that management is more 'in touch' with the situation 'bluffs' are not really possible, if indeed they are at any time; if sanctions are suggested either the claim is settled or the sanctions carried through.

Federal negotiations

The other definitive type of national claim is that pursued through the procedures of an Employers' Federation. There is a marked similarity between the previous types of national case and this type in that both are at the end (or near the end) of procedures and that both have the same pressures forcing the claim towards this stage. There is another form of national claim on an Employers' Federation basis which involves the negotiation of national basic minimum rates, which are 'topped-up' by local-level bargaining. This type of claim is traditional in the construction and farming industries (although the latter shows a marked tendency for the minimum and maximum salaries to coincide) and has been the method used in negotiations between the Engineering Unions and the Engineering Employers' Federation; although in 1972–3 the unions sought to break away into plant by plant bargaining.

In the national minima bargaining case, negotiations are between the most senior union officials and officials of the Federation who, in engineering, are appointed professional-career negotiators. The claim has so far always been for substantially more than the eventual settlement and is sophisticated, and in most cases is the major claim (if not the only one) of the year or two year period. The question of sanctions if raised is not easily answered, because the diversity and multiplicity of plants and unions makes contact between and organisation of members difficult and the Employers' Federation back individual companies through a common pool if guerilla tactics are used. The settlement only produces minima for salaries, holiday entitlements, overtime and shift premia, etc., the actual rate is negotiated at plant or enterprise level and this is dealt with in the following chapter.

Employers' Federations are essentially trade unions of employers and in any negotiations at national level the bargaining is conducted by professionals on either side of the table, who are removed from the individual sites of work and must be mandated by their respective members. This tends to slow down a negotiation as both sides have to report back on any movement in the other's position. In addition to this a ballot or soundings have to be made of the union's members in the event of a settlement in the offing, and the employer's side has to make the same soundings. Efficiency is not at a premium in these instances. The details of Central Conference Federation claims and national-level negotiations based on a plant or area basis are covered in the following chapter as their main characteristics are not set by the officer who negotiates but the character of the claim imposed by a group of employees who work together, live near each other, share common recreation facilities and can predict the effect of a settlement on each other.

National v. local negotiations

Are national negotiations preferable to those conducted at local level? Are they more effective in that better settlements finally emerge? The engineering unions certainly thought not when they tried to get plant-level bargaining instead of their national, minimum-wage negotiations. A totally diverse product or service industry or company does not lend itself to national negotiations in any form, and one can hardly envisage a set of negotiations which covers the insurance workers, artificial-limb fitters, ceramic-tile operatives and truck drivers that all come into the Thomas Tilling Group. One company, ICI, has attempted to create a common job classification for all staff employees across its different product ranges but this worked only because the company unilaterally imposed the classification and the subsequent levels of salary; this has now been changed to collective bargaining. Conversely, national negotiations apply in a single product, single service industry for example British Rail, insurance companies, banking or the Post Office. It can be argued that by negotiating a minimum wage a union takes the pressure off the management and that in these circumstances the actual salary is low. Statistics tend to confirm this view of minimum-level bargaining although there are some exceptions notably that of the printing sectors but, these notwithstanding, agricultural workers, hospital workers and shop workers are all well entrenched in the lower quartiles of salary surveys.

Devolving to local level has its own disadvantages. The logistical problems of such operations are formidable in a large industry or company and the trade union side needs good officer coverage and an articulate, competent and trained membership to cope with the strains. If some local branches are weak or management very strong it is obvious that, overall, the union members could be worse off in these locations than they would have been had they had their salary negotiated in a national agreement. To take this a stage further, if the strength of unions is concentrated in a handful of large areas and the rest dispersed in smaller, weaker groups the majority of union members could lose by using local negotiations. The defenders of local bargaining theorise that this cannot happen because the company or plant paying less will not retain or attract its labour. But this argument assumes full employment and perfect knowledge of employment markets by employees in one discrete area and total mobility of labour between areas. The latter two do not exist, whilst the former occurs only too frequently.

It would seem that both local and national level negotiations have their drawbacks and that, if a choice is available, it must be exercised with care and advantage taken of the prevailing structure of the industry or company. The present negotiating scene in Britain is based on historic factors and in some cases the structure of society has overtaken the methods used. The conglomerate company, based not upon either vertical or horizontal integration but on random profit-making, often short term only, poses a challenge to unions in the negotiating sphere and like the multi-plant, multi-product company would probably be best served by local negotiations but with a provision for central negotiations for any condition on a company-wide basis, for example, a pension scheme. New industries and new technologies will certainly change the structure of collective bargaining; it will have to become more flexible, to deal with the demands made on it by the impact of computerisation, raw material substitutions, an increasingly more sophisticated and better qualified workforce and greater specialisation. It could be that in ten years' time the division between national and local claims will have disappeared for most of the employees in Britain, claims will be made alternatively at different levels for different items or on a trans-national basis.

Chapter 4

Local claims

'To win or lose it all' – James Graham

The bread and butter work

The previous chapter discussed the mechanism of some national negotiations in detail and, in passing, mentioned local claims, especially in the context of Federations or Employers' Associations. The national claim is the one that entices the media, generally an industry-wide claim on behalf of miners or railwaymen or farm labourers, or occasionally in a single, large company such as ICI, Esso or Pilkington. The publicity is wide because the effect of claims is broad; when it is settled it not only costs a lot in money terms due to the sheer weight of numbers of those involved, it also has the effect of changing inter-industry differentials and may be a pace-setting agreement and thus have repercussions outside of the claim in question. It may also, as has happened in the past, prove to be a trial of strength between the unions in question and the government with regard to its incomes policy, or may be seen in these terms. Thus the national claim is the one which the public at large are led to believe is typical of all trade-union bargaining. This is far from being so. The local claim is as important, if not more so, as its 'big brother' with more time and effort being expended at this less-publicised level.

A claim is presented at local level because the procedure agreement dictates that this method should be used. A large, probably multi-product, company with plants scattered around Britain will have its bargaining started at local level as in British Leyland or GEC. A single, small company with only one plant can be rightly said to have both local and 'national' negotiations running simultaneously, but in any industrial-relations vocabulary these are local negotiations. The third type of involvement at this level is the company belonging to an Employers' Federation and this can, of course, in'clude some companies in the above two categories.

By and large, the claim is made at the same intervals as those at national level, at yearly or two-yearly intervals depending on the periodicity of the last agreement. The stages, however, are somewhat different and, as one would expect, there is a far greater involvement at grass-roots levels at all stages of the claim and its subsequent settlement. It is this involvement that makes the determination of attitudes, by both parties, so much easier and gives this level of negotiations its distinctive, but often bitter, flavour.

The impression might have been given in the previous chapter that there is but one claim on an employer per year; this impression must be corrected, especially when discussing this level of bargaining. Although one item, such as the major one of salaries, may only be referred once every year there may also be separate agreements on holidays, bonuses or redundancy compensation and these agreements, and others of their type representing elements in the remuneration package, may have different due dates so that negotiations may be continuing on one subject or another throughout the year. This applies far more to local bargaining where there is easier access to management than at national level where the package tends to be negotiated *in toto*. When discussing the intervals between negotiations and the presentation of the claim this must be borne in mind. The interval is that dictated by the last settlement, affecting only those subjects mentioned in the settlement, and although the gap between presentation of claims is one year this may be at two-monthly intervals each year. Also, negotiations for piece workers, in metalworking industries with product changes, operate almost continuously.

Local claims and changes

Managements do not usually initiate offers: the union takes the initiative and puts in the claim. Initially this is done by the group of workers at the plant in question who delegate the function of putting the claim to management to a representative or a committee of representatives. The meeting is held on company premises, in company time and between the management (represented by members of their personnel or industrial relations department) and the union side. In the larger companies where local negotiations can involve many thousands of employees the union may have a full-time representative, paid by the company, with secretarial assistance and accommodation provided by the company but whose function is to be an exclusively on-site, full-time union representative. Although this may seem a strange thing for a management to spend its money on, it is in the management's interests to have a stable and well-informed unionised workforce and a full-time lay official can act as a prime mover to get to this situation. The last state of affairs an intelligent employer wants to see is fragmentation of his unionised employees with each fragment pulling in differing directions, and concerned say, only with a very small, specialised group of workers, when a small outlay helps him counter this situation. The Employment Protection Act will tend to speed up the establishment of posts like this in new or previously weakly-organised areas of employment.

Many claims are settled at this first stage of negotiations. Management knows the workforce and can easily judge the backing which union members would give to the negotiating committee, thus there is always the possibility of quick settlement. Either a management will make a low counter-offer knowing that no sanctions will be taken and the union will be forced to accept it or it will make a higher counter-offer knowing that failure to agree at this stage will bring in the local professional negotiator and sanctions then appear on the horizon. It is also true that management at a local level are not always pleased when they have to meet a full-time union official. There are many reasons for this; the main one seemingly a strange, psychological desire to keep the dispute 'within the family'. It cannot be stressed strongly enough that, at a local level, the personnel department know the union negotiators in the dual role of employees and bargainers, giving management a distinct psychological edge. A full-time official has no link with that particular company, his promotion does not depend on his behaviour patterns, indeed from the company point of view almost the direct opposite holds. The full-time officer is a professional negotiator and not an employee who volunteers for and has a flair for bargaining. This can have an intimidating influence on a man or woman whose main function is that of personnel officer and to whom collective bargaining is only a small facet of his work. Finally, if a full-time officer is called in it generally pre-supposes that the employees feel strong enough to bargain in earnest – otherwise they would probably have settled at or near the original offer.

The claim presented to management at this stage differs in its level of sophistication dependent upon the ability of the local representatives to formulate a claim and also upon the need. If it is a strongly unionised and experienced group of employees in a high-profile situation the claim is more basic than that of a small group in a service, non-productive or low-profile sector. A basic claim presents the demand or demands, an argument on internal differentials or local, comparable wages and conditions; which may not even be in writing. On a more sophisticated level the claim is presented giving arguments as to the profitability of the concern (or its ability to meet the claim), some national income or price data and a few local comparators. The nature of local claims is such that this is, at most, all that is required, and then only to convince the membership of the rightness of the claim rather than seek to persuade the management. In the preceding chapter we pointed out that logic plays little part in the eventual settlement, but, as there is often a national audience, there is a need to have some impact in the form of a well-written claim. At local level, however, with no critical comment on the sidelines, the matter becomes one of expediency. The union will use its strength, the company its counter-strength and the result will be a deal with the company weighing various factors against each other and the arguments in the claim, however well reasoned they are, are more often than not forgotten. But the base must be rational for the unions must be rational.

Local industrial actions

These factors depend on the type of management, the type of company and the type of union membership. A single-plant company is generally more vulnerable to the thought of industrial action than one plant in a larger, multi-plant company. On the other hand, it is precisely this type of smaller enterprise where unions have often not recruited adequately and whose management feel so personally identified with the plant that any rejection of an offer is taken as a personal affront. The AUEW strike at the small engineering company of Con-Mech is the best example of this, although the strike was over recognition of the union, not an economic issue. This *cause célèbre* when the NIRC confiscated £100,000 of what was really Labour Party money in trust was the subject of a CIR report. In the report the managing director of Con-Mech stated he saw no need for a trade union as both he and other directors occasionally visited the plant and talked to employees. This man was obviously personally identifying with the company and incidentally totally missing the point behind trade unionism; the identification was carried to its extreme when he rejected the CIR report and refused to allow recognition to the AUEW. This makes two points, first, the difficulty is getting recognition in this sort of situation and second, that resistance is partly based on both fear of the unknown and the realisation that the company would be vulnerable in negotiations. Output lost in a single-plant enterprise cannot be transferred to another plant, or indeed another country, as so often happens with larger concerns. This however needs to be qualified.

A single plant in a multi-plant complex may not have the problem of lost output in quite the same manner, but at the same time, may actually be more at risk. If the parent company has many plants which duplicate the goods or services there is a lessening of the pressure upon the plant – a low-profile situation; if the plant is producing goods or services which are not so replaceable we have a high-profile situation. If the end product is also either a vital intermediate product within the parent company's vertically-integrated system or is an intermediate product within an external chain the profile climbs to Everest proportions. A management thus has to weigh its own internal possibilities and capabilities against the probability of industrial action if satisfactory settlement terms are not offered, the difference between this and the national level claim being twofold. A management at local level knows the mood of its employees far better than reports back from branches to head office can inform a national industrial relations executive; decisions on the management side are thus taken in the light of fuller information. Conversely the union side at local level has the local social pattern re-inforcing the appeals for solidarity, canvassing opinion is easier and the result more accurate, and thus a confrontation, should there be one, is generally based on either prejudice or miscalculation by the management side.

Having stated this, there is the odd occasion when a company just cannot afford to pay increases but where the union side does not believe this to be true, believing the company to be 'crying wolf' just once too often. The classic example here was a six-month strike of draughtsmen at Rolls-Royce just prior to the crash. However the management had not been disclosing all the data.

If the foregoing seems to have an unhealthy pre-occupation with industrial actions – which reinforces all pre-conceived ideas about trade-unions, consider the following points. At a local level the employer has a considerable impact on the percentage of unemployment, total purchasing power and general prosperity of shopkeepers, estate agencies and professional workers in the vicinity and without a trade union there would be no countervailing pressure. Indeed one can go as far as to argue that solicitors, dentists, all the service industry proprietors, the local chamber of commerce and all those who have not traditionally been allied to the trade-union movement should support a trade union in local negotiations for their increasing prosperity depends on the ability of the union to get the customers or clients their salary increases. If a local employer has the power of hire and fire, should not employees in a local situation, have the right to either withdraw their labour or refuse to work excessive hours? Most of the time the question of industrial action is academic, but if it were not in the background what incentive other than recruitment or retaining of staff would a management have to improve the wages and conditions of their employees? In a local situation an employer is often in a monopolistic situation as far as employment is concerned especially as specialisation continues apace. His recruitment is a small problem and he can manipulate wage levels and personnel numbers relatively easily in a non-union situation. The theory of labour markets is, as explained earlier, an imperfect one in all senses.

If no settlement is arrived at after negotiations between the local management and the local full-time official, one of two things will happen. There will be either a dispute or, if the procedure agreement stipulates, a national official of the union will continue negotiations with senior executives at plant level or with the parent company's industrial relations department. This extra stage is more meaningful than the 'national' stage in an Employers' Federation procedure and often leads to settlements of one description or another. This is probably due as much to the change of style in the negotiators and their increased discretionary powers as it is to their expertise, but for whatever reasons, settlements are often hammered out in the last stages.

The previous chapters have mentioned and discussed Employers' Federations and there is sometimes difficulty in tidily classifying negotiations here. The national minima negotiation is, of course, a purely national claim and negotiation but individual plant negotiations should be seen to be local even when pursued through to a Central Conference or national level. Employers' associations differ in their internal organisation and recommended procedures but again let us take the Engineering Employers' Federation as an example.

Local negotiations and employers' federations

The Engineering Employers' Federation is a Federation of local Engineering Employers' Associations (in the same way that the National Union of Mineworkers is a federation of NUM areas): both having local autonomy but capable of acting on a national basis as a coherent unit. Companies can become members of the EEF but only on the basis of where they have their plant, so, for example, the British Aircraft Corporation plant in Bristol is a member of the South West Association whilst the Burnley plant is a member of Lancashire Association. The Federation recognises certain unions at national level. For specified groups of employees recognition automatically follows at local level – except the managers who are dealt with on an *ad hoc* basis.

The Federation does not impose local procedure agreements on their member companies but once a procedure has been accepted by both the Federation and the union, for national processing of claim, each company's agreements are deemed to contain the same stages even if certain specific local variants are written in. Again the Federation does not seek to impose a precise bargaining policy on its member Associations but it does make recommendations, as for example, in November 1973 it circulated all member companies to the effect that they should not negotiate 'threshold agreements' under Phase III. The way the system works is theoretically to devolve negotiations and decisions to local levels – though in practice, a multi-plant company will tend to try to impose a common-response pattern to similar claims made in different Association areas, allowing only for the flexibility inherent in a local bargaining system.

The procedure is as follows: representatives of the union meet the company and put the claim, if there is no settlement a full-time union official meets the company. If this does not settle the matter a Local Conference is called. Here representatives of the local Engineering Employers' Association meet in the Association Offices along with the management, the full-time official and the lay representatives of the union. Negotiations take place at this meeting which is chaired by an official of the Employers' Association. The procedure at the meeting varies from Association to Association but basically the union official puts his case. The management-cum-Association then retire to discuss the matter and return with a reply, occasionally 'yes', more often a counter-offer, occasionally 'no', although this depends on the claim and the conditions. If no settlement is reached a 'failure to agree' is registered and a Central Conference hearing is fixed. Central Conference is the final stage of the Engineering Employers' Federation Procedure and has been traditionally held in York or London depending on the unions involved.

If a procedure were to be devised with the dual aims of slowing negotiations and avoiding settlements whilst maximising the ritual aspect, the authors need look no further than the Engineering Employers' Federation – in an industry which has an unenviable record of disputes. The first problem is that procedure has to be exhausted. This alone means that the hopeless cases usually arrive at Central Conference both sides realising that if the cases were capable of being settled this would have been done at local conference or earlier. Such cases may be referred back to local level, in others a 'failure to agree' is registered but both parties realise that in this instance no action will be taken. Second, cases which would have been settled at the Local Conference stage are pursued through to National Level because one or both sides think something may come out of it to their advantage, which it seldom if ever does, however the fact it is *available* delays the settlement. Finally, in almost every case, either an adjournment, a reference back or a 'failure to agree' is registered, because attitudes on both sides have become fixed.

The procedure at Central Conference is significantly different to that of Local Conferences. The theory is that parties who have had no involvement in any of the preceding stages will, by logical arguments, be able to settle a disputed claim, where others with direct contacts and positions to protect have failed. Thus the negotiations are between the Federation employees and the national officials of the union with adjournments available for both sides to consult with their members. At no time will the company or employees be directly concerned with the negotiations. Occasionally the negotiations are mercifully quick. For example, an employer–chairman has been known to say to a union official 'Are you in a yes or no mood?' 'Yes' and then 'no' here meaning an end of negotiation resulting in a 'failure to agree'. Although the five-second negotiation is the exception rather than the rule the theory of disinterested settlement does not work in practice and, in truth, the five-second negotiation is often worthwhile. The problem is that neither side are disinterested. The Federation can only advise its member company which has by now an entrenched position and the same, though to a far less-marked degree applies to the union side. Equally important is that both sides are in a real sense negotiating by proxy, rather like proposing marriage through an intermediary and the resulting consummations are as rare.

'Failures to agree' fall into two categories. Those which result from exhausting the procedure and those which result from genuine differences. In the former case the claim is either dropped until the next negotiation or resubmitted through procedure almost immediately, often in a slightly different guise, the latter generally means an industrial dispute is brewing unless for tactical reasons this is not pursued. Although this form of claim sounds a waste of time the Engineering Employers' Federation, has provided and continues to provide stability in industrial relations and a useful framework for negotiations covering three million workers, the main problem being the ritual waste of time going to the Central Conference stage.

The special flavour of local negotiations

Local negotiations or 'domestic claims' are the most personalised aspect of negotiations and for much of the time they deal not in economic claims but in disputes as to grievance procedures, dismissals, work practices, etc. It is here that a union representative does his, or her, main work, taking up cases on behalf of aggrieved individuals or objecting to some introductions of work techniques. Both the union representatives and the appropriate company negotiator come to know each other over time, recognising foibles and being able to predict, with surprising accuracy, the reactions of one to the other's statements or actions. If an employer knows that the union representative is consistent in his attitudes and vice versa then no matter that each thinks the other incorrigible, life for all situations can be made tolerable. However, when either a change of policy or inconsistency creeps in the situation can become soured. Consistency has enormous merit in well-established relationships.

One permanently annoying part of the collective bargaining scene has been the public posturing of politicians which is annoying not in the abstract but to the party who has been the subject of the abuse. This is a national claim phenomenon, especially where governments are concerned. The 'settle or I will call an early election' syndrome is calculated to harden the union's attitude and make a settlement far more difficult to reach, as is the 'traitors to Britain' ploy, or in the private sector 'ruining the industry' or 'we will invest in South Africa or Spain in future'. These statements are political platforms which ignore the causes of the dispute and are intended to impress those outside of the industry or company as to the courage, hardness or power of the management side. Fortunately, the local negotiation is relatively free of this vexatious habit for the obvious reason that few people outside the immediate area will be interested, thus the annoyances will be on a personal level rather than the national publicity level.

The settlement at local level is no different from that at national level except that there are fewer potential anomalies. A local negotiation can take local conditions into account whilst a national negotiation has to be based on the premise that employees have the same problems in all parts of the country and special local factors can only be taken into account in the context of the major agreement, for example London Weighting Allowances. An example of this is British Rail. Drivers get a bonus dependent upon the length of journey, for example London–Edinburgh attracts a larger bonus than Bristol–Birmingham. This means that Southern Region (the busiest in the world) with its plethora of short, commuter journeys gives a train driver less income than the inter-city driver. Yet the London–Edinburgh driver may live in Edinburgh where the cost of living is far lower than in London or its environs where the Southern Region driver must live. This is one reason why the Southern

Region drivers are so militant. The negotiating procedure discriminates against them and a regionally-based procedure would be the more attractive.

Whether local or national claims are the ones of choice was discussed in the previous chapter, but as we can now see they are very different in character and the choice can determine the final settlement. From a trade union point of view, if the success of a claim is dependent on the skill of the negotiator, the national system is preferable to the local, as more members will be covered by the more skilled and experienced officials; on the other hand speed, flexibility and knowledge are lost. Two-tier systems can be devised and these are probably the best method for combining local and national systems but in the last analysis industrial development, technology and trade union growth and survival will determine the structure of negotiations in the future. Whatever choice is made, one thing is certain, employees and trade unions must be allowed to freely negotiate their salaries, conditions of service and work conditions in a system which allows them to use their collective weight in a precise and collective fashion. It is less inflationary and certainly more democratic.

Chapter 5

Arbitration

'I will be conquered, I will not capitulate' – Johnson

What is arbitration?

When two parties in a dispute are incapable of arriving at a settlement and when all rational arguments, persuasions, analogues and
threats have been exhausted, one way out of the impasse is to submit
the dispute to arbitration. This is not necessarily exclusive to the
practice of industrial relations; arbitration is used far more widely
in contractual disputes between commercial parties and in the
avoidance of law-suits than it ever has been in a wage bargaining
sense. The arbiter is a member of an old and honoured profession.
Who amongst us has not seen at least one filmed Biblical epic which
has a scene of parties in a dispute, generally over land or the only
available starlet, going out of the village to a small stream-side hut
where an old man listens to both sides and delivers his instant
judgment, impartial, wise and acceptable to all. Idealised it may
be, but based on the inescapable truth that when all else fails,
groups in differing societies have turned either to conciliation, the
detached arbiter or have made war.

Disputes which have not been settled by other means occasionally
become the subject of arbitration in the collective bargaining world.
It is only an occasional happening because most unions and managements settle their disputes without such recourse and because the
procedure agreements within which they operate do not have an
arbitration clause. Nevertheless, there are times when this procedure is useful in all manner of disputes. There are many types of
cases in which arbitration may be used, ranging from a disagreement
over a claim on salaries and conditions to industrial disciplinary
cases, technical judgments on productivity schemes or the settlement
of an intractable dispute situation.

In an earlier chapter a procedure agreement which ended with an
arbitration clause (especially an automatic one) was described as one

negotiated out of relative weakness. If a trade union's bargaining position is such that at the end of the day it cannot deliver what it claims to its members but must rely on an outside compromise it does not argue from a position of strength. If an agreement has a terminal clause involving arbitration the incentive for either side to settle at the earlier stages is lessened because, assuming that the arbiter is independent, the probability is that the verdict will be a compromise offering comfort and castor-oil to both sides in relatively equal measures. Why spoil so amicable an arrangement by agreeing to accept a compromise so near to the mid-point? One of the sides will always lose something by doing so. This argument does not assume that arbitration will always tend to the mid-point position, it assumes that both sides think it will do so; the thought is almost synonymous with arbitration. The wish is however father to the thought. In fact many decisions come down heavily on one of the sides, often because insufficient care has been exercised in the choosing of the arbiter, or the terms of reference have not been fully understood, vetted or the case presented has been conspicuously poor either in itself or in the presentation.

The procedural arbitration clause

Let us first examine some of the different cases which can become the subject of arbitration. The first is the case mentioned above, the last stage of a procedure agreement. This used to be prevalent among the weaker unions in the white-collar field, whose members would not under any circumstances (or so their unions once believed) take industrial action in the furtherance of their claims. In a salary-and-conditions claim, well-researched and sophisticated arguments backed by impeccable logic have more effect on the membership making the claim than on the management. The unions which consistently negotiate 'arbitration agreements' have little faith in either their members or their ability to produce such a claim and thus convince the members of the overwhelming righteousness of their case. However this is all changing once such a conviction has taken hold and even civil servants have been known to take action. Conversely, such a claim is unlikely to impress an employer in quite the same manner; the employer has to pay if he is impressed by pressure. In cases of procedural arbitration the union that has negotiated the procedural agreement generally describes the system as one which is redolent of old fashioned 'responsible' trade unionism.

This essentially social and argumentative proposition can and must be investigated as it raises fundamental questions about the whole collective bargaining system in Britain. To whom or what is a trade union responsible for there to be such an approach as 'responsible trade unionism'? If a union is responsible to its members in that the democratic systems within the union are functioning properly, with the members paying their subscriptions, the main responsibility must not only be to the members but *they* must also take responsibility. The negotiating officials on the union's staff are in duty bound to represent the interests of their members in a way similar to that in which managers of a company are responsible to, and represent the interests of the shareholders although this is a far more distant relationship. The 'responsible trade union' argument is often used to mean trade unions agreeing with employers on all matters after taking into account a higher and frequently redefined 'national interest'. This concept has been the subject of countless political science and philosophy treatises and to try to discuss it again in this book would be without gain. Nevertheless, even if it exists in a capitalist system, surely a union has no such responsibility. No one talks of a 'responsible company' because it is accepted that some form of profit or sales optimisation for the benefit of the holders of its equity is its *raison d'etre*. The argument is totally one-sided and is politically inspired, to put no finer point on it. A responsible trade union is one which negotiates the best possible terms and conditions of service and represents the interests of its members in the most effective way. It may be that to do this through arbitration on a procedural basis is the alternative of choice; it may not be and the responsible action would be to take industrial action. Each case, each employer, each membership is specific to the negotiations at hand and must be treated as such.

Exhausted procedure

A second reason for having an arbiter on a salaries and conditions claim is in a situation where although procedure has been exhausted, no settlement has taken place; general industrial action has been undertaken, resources and/or the solidarity of the claimants is running down or the management cannot withstand the pressure any longer. A recent well-known example of this was the 'arbitration' by the Wilberforce Enquiry after the strike called by the National Union of Mineworkers in January 1972. The strike and its associated picketing proved remarkably successful in an economic sense and after one month the Government declared a state of emergency followed by the appointment of a Court of Enquiry. The enquiry was headed by Sir William Wilberforce assisted by Mr John Garnett of the Industrial Society and Professor Hunter of Glasgow University.

Although it was the Government which intervened in this instance due to a national fuel crisis and an attendant inherent public sympathy for the case of the miners, smaller local disputes, as opposed to nationally paralysing ones, often end in a similar enquiry by mutual agreement of the parties. In this case mutual agreement was unlikely because the solidarity of the miners on their first national strike since 1926 was undiminished after four weeks and they played the dominant role in economic and social terms: it was not a stalemate position. The enquiry could only recommend certain actions. The NUM made it clear that a ballot would have to be taken of all members to call off the strike and therefore they could not be bound by the results of the investigation. Evidence was given by both sides to the Court of Enquiry in the normal way and in public.

The Wilberforce Enquiry was a true arbitration but not one binding on the parties. The awards made were a compromise between the claimed increases and the final offer, viz., underground workers received an increase of £6 per week although the final offer had been £3.56 per week. Both sides accepted the Enquiry team as impartial and a settlement was achieved (albeit with some additional last-minute concessions made at a high political level). The fact that it was a Court of Enquiry does not disqualify it from being described as an arbitration. The test is in the terms of reference under which the Enquiry takes place; these may be wide-ranging social and political or closely defined to achieve a specific purpose as with Wilberforce. The purpose was to end the dispute and the reference was to make an award, i.e., to arbitrate between the miners and the National Coal Board. An arbitration by any other name. . . .

Arbitration can take place in the full glare of public attention as in the case of the Wilberforce Enquiry and, as with arbitrations on national disputes, especially in or after dispute situations. The majority of arbitrations however occur quietly and locally, in a no-less partisan or occasionally bitter atmosphere, but as part of the bread and butter of industrial relations rather than the icing on a television news programme. The arbitration of technical issues represents a large percentage of these cases.

Technical and personal arbitration

Technical subjects in this context are not about the nozzle-guide vanes on jet engines, they are the structuring of staff patterns, efficiency and productivity schemes, job-evaluation proposals and all their associated, specialised management techniques. When confronted with a disagreement on such issues, the arguments, although the issues are often ones of principle, tend to be technical and jargon-ridden. A union in negotiations on these matters can, if it is not careful, be misled by facile, simplistic explanations of new techniques which, if implemented, would operate to their members' disadvantage. The fact that the explanations are complicated mitigates against managing to convince members that industrial action is necessary and in any event, if members cannot assess the case in detail they are loath to take sharp action. If an impasse results, arbitration is the best solution by providing a cool atmosphere to develop detailed arguments that might otherwise be lost in the heat of battle.

Personal grievances are often the most eligible for investigation and report. A classic case was the Ford worker dismissed allegedly for striking a foreman. The worker claimed he did not do so; his union supported him and a prolonged stoppage resulted. An extra-procedural arbitration was agreed and in a compromise the worker was re-employed in another department and the dispute settled. It is not always necessary for a dispute to occur before arbitration takes place; a wise management will take this course of action to defuse a potentially difficult situation and yet save face.

The case might centre around a plant where a union is building up strength but as yet has no formal recognition. The main union activist might then be dismissed on either trivial grounds or on fictitious charges. A dispute then follows which has the dual aim of re-instating the union activist and, in addition, securing the recognition of the union. Not unnaturally this can become difficult to unravel and positions become firmly entrenched in that 'face-saving' is the management priority while survival becomes the union objective. Investigative arbitration can be effective in such cases.

To bind or not to bind

It is not uncommon for a third party to set the scene for an arbitration hearing, especially in cases involving a work stoppage. We have seen that the Government actually intervenes in some cases which it considers to be of national importance. The Department of Employment conciliation department which carried the burden before the establishment of the Advisory Conciliation and Arbitration Service (the Department, ACAS and CAC naturally maintain lists of suitably-qualified mediators) used to try to get the two sides to agree on such a course. The TUC were instrumental in setting up the arbitration at Ford's in October 1973 and the non-arbitration Court of Enquiry at Chrysler's (which arbitrated) also in October 1973.

The stage is set for the discussion of the technique of arbitration hearings but for one point. To obey the findings of the arbiter or not? If the procedure agreement stipulates arbitration it is often explicit that the arbiters findings are binding, if not it is certainly implicit. If the arbitration is extra-procedural no such constraints exist. In the Wilberforce Enquiry the National Union of Mineworkers were constitutionally unable to move prior to a ballot of their membership and in many dispute situations a vote or ballot is necessary to terminate the dispute and thus accept an arbitration award. Management has no such difficulty yet will often give no guarantee of accepting the decision and, for example, in a Spennymoor case Courtaulds refused to implement the decisions. In general this is unusual for both sides if only because of the time lapse between the inception of the idea and the decision; this can run into months which, more than anything, defuses the situation.

One specific form of award must be observed when handed down. Inter-union disputes, once the subject of bitter disagreements are now mainly settled by a TUC internal arbitration method based on principles arrived at at the Hull, Bridlington and Croydon Congresses. This 'Bridlington' machinery works through a prior notification and consent system up to a full three-man 'Disputes Committee' which hears the complaint. The Chairman is a TUC General Council member and his Committee's findings are mandatory on the participants. The system is genuinely an arbitrational one in that the Chairman is independent of the two sides, both give evidence, the decision is taken and normally complied with. In a classic case, the union concerned left the TUC and has not rejoined. There are also informal hearings on potential problems chaired by a General Council member without 'sidemen'.

Pre-arbitration choices

When an arbitration is to take place the first two fundamental decisions to be made are the selection of the arbiter(s) and the terms of reference of the arbitration. Selecting the arbiter can be as difficult and prolonged as the original contentious process. There are several methods of selection. A procedure agreement arbitration often specifically nominates the organisation from whom the arbiter will be chosen. ACAS or the Industrial Society are the favourites. The agreement may stipulate the profession of the arbiter as does the Productivity Scheme agreement between the Prudential and ASTMS (in that case an accountant). Other agreements have no such specification or the arbitration is an extra-procedural response to a difficult situation. In such cases an arbiter must be conjured out of thin air.

The difficulty in the selection is that both sides want to have an arbiter who they think will be at least emotionally on their side if not totally committed to their fundamental point of view. Correspondingly, both sides take great care in seeing that the other party does not gain an advantage. A generally recognised method is to have an outside body appoint the arbiter. This used to be done by the Department of Employment when their conciliation department arranged arbitration hearings. Now that the Government has relinquished this task to ACAS the same approach applies. If no outside body is materialised to impose the choice of an arbiter the two sides generally swap lists of three or four likely people and from these the arbiter is chosen by mutual consent and generally on the principle of minimisation of disadvantage. In each list there is generally at least one candidate totally favourable to the side which submitted his name and the others grade into impartiality. The ploy is obviously to reject the anti-union candidate and the first step is to identify him (not always as easy as it sounds). Obviously the chairman of a public company in the affected industry would not be acceptable. But academics, lawyers or public or private agency employees can be more mysterious. Contrary to public opinion there are very right-wing academic economists or industrial-relations specialists and they are not always sympathetic. Those with a known public history are easy to spot but those with apparently unimpeachable qualifications, whose publications have appeared in obscure journals, can be difficult to spot; motives are harder still.

Let us assume that an arbiter has been chosen, acceptable to both sides – a well-known, impartial academic. There is, incidentally, an Institute of Arbiters who, for a fee, will provide names and backgrounds of arbiters but it seems not to have been used by trade unions. One way of ensuring against eccentric personal views is to provide for two assessors to assist the chairman, who can be nominated by either side without challenge. The next decision to be taken is on the terms of reference of the arbitration. This decision is as important as the choice of arbiter as both can influence the final decision. There are two features to watch for. The first is the introduction of an external consideration into the reference. For example the arbiter could be asked to decide on the merits of a specific case *but* in the light of the 'public interest'. This is a favourite government ploy and automatically assures that the only winner will be the government as by definition it is assumed only the government can define the phrase 'common interest'. The 'common interest' or 'public interest' or 'common good' are merely different ways of describing changing government policies. Other issues that can be introduced are 'subject to the state of the economy' or 'subject to the state of the market', constraints which really mean 'disregard the justice of the case and find against the union'.

The second pitfall to avoid is more general in its application, less overt in presentation and more subtle in effect. It is less a single pitfall than a family of trip-wires. An arbitration follows on some form of dispute and each dispute has a history of its own and often has more than one ramification. The terms of reference must address themselves to the main point or points of contention, if necessary including the historical background. They must not be side-tracked into peripheral areas, which will force an arbiter to make recommendations on six or so major points and thus dilute the effectiveness of his report. An example is in a technical arbitration on a productivity scheme. It may be that three quarters of the scheme is not in dispute and thus the arbitration should specifically be concerned with the other 25 per cent. If the whole scheme is included in the reference the arbiter's report would be three quarters in favour of the scheme (at least) and the ultimate pressure to amend the other quarter correspondingly reduced. Another example would be an arbitration after a prolonged strike on salaries involving large sums of potential back pay. In such a case the terms of reference must be totally specific; to determine the correct salary for that group of workers, and that alone. The 'rightness' of the dispute or the back pay are both irrelevant as is an examination of conditions at the plants. More than one decision has been unsatisfactory because the terms of reference were far too wide. The major problem can be diluted in a supersaturated solution of irrelevancies.

Preparing and presenting the case

So far then, the arbiter has been chosen, the terms of reference have been decided, both in a short space of time, and a convenient date for the hearing is fixed. It is useful to have enough time to prepare a detailed case to present to the arbitrator even if, as is normal this necessitates long hours of work in a short time. Although arbitrations have oral hearings some arbiters insist on, others prefer, and most welcome a written statement of case either before the hearing or as an *aide-mémoire* during their deliberations. Arbitration hearings are mostly held in private with only the interested parties present, although some with a national flavour have been held in public. The privacy guarantees that rhetoric is kept to a minimum and that the case is presented as logically and succinctly as possible because there is no capital to be made from political or emotive statements. Both sides normally exchange their written submissions at least three days before the hearing opens.

No two cases for arbitration are the same. The differences are more marked than in negotiation claims because the internal structure of the concern plays a larger part. When preparing a case it must be firmly recognised that it is built around and tailored to the terms of reference. An arbiter would be quite within his rights to ignore the irrelevant, however much the presenter of the argument is persuaded of its truth. It is possible of course to introduce side issues, personality problems and clashes in the building up of a logical proposition aimed at one of the terms of the reference. All these gambits tarnish the process but they exist and are used.

The case is different to that prepared for a claim, for negotiations will play no part in the outcome and no-one has to be persuaded except the arbiter(s). As seen earlier, a claim is intended to have as much effect on the membership as it has on the employer; an arbitration case is aimed solely at the arbiter in order to get the most favourable decision possible. When the background of the arbiter is known it is possible to present the arguments in a way that will appeal to him, for example if the arbiter is an accountant it is useful to have an accountant either brief the officer presenting the case or have an accountant present on the Union side. This is not only a matter of 'jargonising' but an appeal to the internal logic and thought processes that the arbiter has acquired in his training and in his job.

Cases must be prepared very thoroughly and treated essentially as a presentation before a court. The initial statement must be a detailed and accurate history of the dispute, the bringing out the salient features, giving participant's names, dates, times and places. A technical arbitration need not necessarily have this introduction as *these* pieces of data are generally not in dispute. The basic difference between a technical and industrial dispute-solving arbitration is that the former is generally fought on a conceptual basis whilst the latter may not only have differing interpretations of facts but the facts themselves generally may be in dispute. When used, the history should be sparse, contain no elaboration and be capable of resisting challenge by the opposing party; it can be jarring or even disastrous to include erroneous statements; the maxim must be 'if in doubt leave it out'.

The second section should be the statement of case using the history but applying it to the problem at hand. If it is a victimisation case, union activities, recruitment, union head office policy are all built around the facts. It is of no value inserting an attributed statement which cannot be documented or substantiated; 'Mr X said he would "get Charley Y if it was the last thing he did" ' is an average and notorious example. An arbiter rightly looks on a report which contains such a statement in the same light as a jury now approaches the verbal statement of a defendant at a police station of 'I did it, it was a fair cop.' It must be remembered that every statement and every fact can be challenged by the opposing party and that the arbiter should get his total knowledge of the facts from the written case and evidence. Thus the case has to be accurate and yet detailed enough to give the arbiter a flavour of the dispute; to appeal to his senses as well as his critical faculties. All documents, minutes, memoranda and letters which are referred to in the case must be numbered and submitted as an appendix to the case. Although rules of evidence do not apply in an arbitration and documents or evidence can generally be produced at the time of the hearing this is a dubious tactic. The advantage is that the opposing party, having no foreknowledge of the point may be temporarily lost but all too often they advance the point into areas not in their submission and the union side is lost, and worse, is seen to be frail, early on.

A technical arbitration poses different problems for a trade union. The first is that the agreement is generally concerned with a company proposal and the initiative is with the company – the onus is on the union not only to demolish the proposal but to present a realistic alternative. Because the proposal emanates from the company it must be assumed that the management has the relevant expertise on tap whilst this may not be true of the union side, whose objections may be more of a philosophic than a technical nature; this is a second problem. There is no reason why, in specific circumstances, a union cannot 'buy in' expert help, an accountant, a management consultant, an organisation and method specialist, because there is equally no reason why a union should not have these professions represented amongst their full-time officials in the field and in the head office staff appointments. In a technical subject, failure to do this could well result in the arbitration going by default and this can hardly be construed as providing a good service to members. Expertise must be matched.

Trade union officials have the reputation of being more than adequate in personal confrontations but less effective at the written side of their work. In this facet of collective bargaining it is as important to be literate and occasionally (in a technical case) numerate as it is to be verbally competent. Points made across a bargaining table with industrial power at the elbow are inappropriate or useless in the arbitration case; debating skill is not at a premium either; what is needed is a cool method of presenting a complicated case simply and an ability to analyse and undermine the opposing party's case.

The decision

After the arbitration comes the arbiter's decision and the central question here is whether the findings are binding and, if so, on whom. The time from the end of the enquiry to the issuing of the report can be considerable depending on complexities of the case and at times the personal commitments of the arbiter and in this time the dispute is normally, as it were, frozen. Most commonly, however, workers will have returned to work when there is a reference to arbitration. If there is no procedural or other formal agreement to abide by the arbiter's decision this time can be used to trace all the alternatives or plan strategies, but by and large the decision is binding in one way or another. The reasons for it being so are compelling. The arbitration would not have been held if there were chances of the dispute being settled by other means or the subject was complex enough to preclude any such actions because it was little understood. The exception to this is where the Government intervenes in a dispute situation which is affecting its concept of the 'national interest' and the dispute is not called off for the duration of the hearing. In this case a union may find it more profitable to continue the dispute. However public opinion marshalled by the media sometimes forecloses on this theoretically profitable manoeuvre. An employer may not find himself bound by the report and indeed it is the employer who is the more likely to accept the findings but not implement them. This has happened after a Department of Employment sponsored arbitration in a Courtaulds plant involving a strike, victimisation and redundancy situation. The arbiter made several proposals none of which were implemented and indeed the management overtly stated that they would not do so.

The growing future of arbitration

At least one trade union leader has seen the future of industrial relations in Britain resting in the hands of a National Arbitration Board. The concept is to remove the threat of industrial action or a lock-out (nowadays a redundancy threat) from the negotiations and replace it with a national system of argument. This method suffers from several drawbacks. There are not enough arbiters of proven ability who are acceptable to both sides. The concept is not unlike the original Commission of Industrial Relations and this was not a signal success although it did achieve settlements on occasions. The idea is to make the Board's reports non-binding but as we have seen it is only the fact that there are no alternatives left that makes for a voluntary acceptance of arbitration decisions and there would always be the alternative of some form of industrial action. The concept assures that industrial relations are carried out in the best of all possible worlds where neither nineteenth century employers nor fringe militants exist. Finally it throws away the trump card a union has to play; its collectivity its solidarity, and its imagination in creating new horizons.

There is a place for arbitration in collective bargaining but that is not in the centre of the top table. It has its uses when all else fails or when nothing else will do. It can resolve a dispute or leave both sides unsatisfied, thus creating trouble for the future. It takes time, consumes expertise and should be used sparingly.

This is written in advance of the cases that will eventually end up at the Central Arbitration Committee set up under the Employee Protection legislation. This can hear unilaterally referred claims against employers who refuse to bargain in situations where ACAS has ordered in favour of union recognition or where a company is not observing the usual terms and conditions for similar employees in a given trade or area. These awards will be legally binding and different in type from those discussed in this chapter, along with Fair Wages Resolution arbitrations. These will be cases taken under Schedule 11 of the Act and will be discussed in chapter eleven of this book.

Chapter 6

The legal processes

'All is Love yet all is Law' – Browning

Early legal difficulties

In an earlier chapter we discussed the recent legislation affecting collective bargaining and sketched some of the cases in which trade unions were involved due to the Industrial Relations Act. This has been altered radically in the field of employee-protection legislation by the initiatives of the 1974 Labour Government. Trade unions have always been involved with the law and generally the law has not treated them with favour. Modern collective bargaining is now more legally orientated than at any previous time. Where, in the past, it was the fundamental right of belonging to a union that was in question and whether certain acts were illegal or not, nowadays it is in the everyday acts of recognition and negotiating that the legal processes play a part. The Heath Government's Industrial Relations Act certainly questioned and constrained certain activities that the trade union movement thought were settled as rights after a century of struggle. The Act was planned to wound the trade union movement but it was one of the most badly-drafted pieces of legislation ever to pass the scrutiny of the House of Commons. Its function was to ensure that the fight between employers and union was re-weighted, and heavily in favour of the employers. This was not an effective gambit because it was out of joint with the times. The General Elections it helped to precipitate have given rise to, in a shorter time than anticipated, more helpful legislation about going to work.

From their earliest days trade unions have had to survive employer-inspired laws which were either aimed at preventing trade union membership or specific union activities. The Combination Acts, conspiracy laws and the Protection of Property Acts all played their part in partially suppressing unions and, more

78

importantly, where other Acts were ambiguous on this point the judiciary interpreted them in line with the policies of those who appointed them. The Tolpuddle Martyrs should be as famous for being the victims of an appalling miscarriage of justice coupled with high political conspiracy, as they are for being trade union martyrs. The point is that over the years it is difficult to find judges whose interpretation of the laws favoured the trade union movement on matters of central principle. The laws on picketing and their interpretation are an illuminating example of this phenomenon.

Pickets

Peaceful picketing has been protected by law since the 1906 Trades Disputes Acts, but successive generations of politicians and lawyers have used other Acts to seek to ban or limit picketing of any description. The current position appears to be that although the now-repealed Industrial Relations Act permitted peaceful picketing it also made it an unfair industrial practice in certain circumstances. Now it seems the law also appears to define picketing as obstruction of the highway if the pickets are stationary or moving. If the police ask a picket either to move or remain stationary and he refuses, it becomes an obstruction of the police in the furtherance of their duty. The present Lord Chief Justice when a High Court Judge ruled that pickets had no more right to use the public highways than a man carrying an advertisement for patent medicine. We now apparently have a situation where peaceful picketing is permitted by the law providing you don't picket.* Fortunately for the order of society most Chief Constables do not encourage the arrest of peaceful pickets. Another example of the use of law in this way was that of a leafleting campaign in the City of London which went to the City Police for approval; they refused on the grounds that it would be conducive to littering by the recipients and the leafleteers might be open to prosecution. Again fortunately they changed their minds, fortunately, as the union concerned intended to challenge this interpretation of legal responsibility by prosecuting a shop owner on the ground his plate-glass window constituted a temptation for brick-throwers. Why then should a trade union even countenance using the legal machinery if both the legislation and its interpretation seem so firmly stacked against them? The answer, in short, is that it should be used if no other method is practicable and the law offers some hope of success and some hope is better than none at all.

---

* As at February 1976 the picketing clauses were omitted from the Employee Protection Bill and are not in the Act and the argument is again in limbo.

Use of legal machinery

The cases where a union generally 'goes to law' are not those which involve the matters of principle to which the previous section referred, except of course, the Heath Government's Industrial Relations Act cases. Unions take up cases on behalf of members in industrial injury situations as a routine service. Most of these never actually reach a court and are settled beforehand but many have been pursued, sometimes to the House of Lords. Other problems involving individual members are breaches of contract, charges of incompetence resulting in damage to property or persons; patent law disputes where a member feels he has been improperly treated and a host of civil actions which can stem from incidents at the work place or on the highway to and from work or in the course of work.

In all the above cases a solicitor must be instructed, and, if felt necessary, a barrister's opinion sought, following which he might be retained for the action. Most unions have a legal department but few employ a solicitor on a full-time basis. Most retain the services of large companies which specialise in handling trade union cases. The procedure is for the member or (in the case of a dependant) the full-time union official on his or her behalf to contact the legal department of the union. This usually acts as a sieve in the process of deciding whether the problem can be solved in ways which do not involve the solicitors. If it is decided to proceed legally the case and all supporting documents are forwarded to the solicitor who then advises on whether it is worth proceeding with, i.e. whether there is a reasonable chance of success. It is at this point that a decision is taken on whether the solicitors may approach a barrister and the member is informed. Normally, if the decision is not to proceed the union's legal department reviews the case and may ask for proceedings to be instagated regardless of the advice, or it may inform the member that there is no chance of success and that if he (or she) is determined to take action it will be on the basis of personal responsibility.

This sort of service is very valuable to members – to whom the courts represent a remote and intimidating process. Bagehot once observed that the panoply and ritual of government was essential as it instilled a feeling of awe and respectfulness amongst the population. The law has traditionally deployed the instruments of ritual: robes, processions and separate language. It has not been exposed to television and therefore the aura of mystery and fear remains for the working-class plaintiff. If the unions did not provide sympathetic (and free) legal services it is unlikely that most members would initiate the proceedings themselves and would thus

abandon their rights. This is compounded by the fact that many
cases have to be initiated when the member is at his lowest ebb, as a
sick or injured person or, in the case of a deceased member, the
dependants under grief. Not all cases brought under this section are
straightforward because both industrial injuries and industrial
diseases are often difficult to establish in a court. The burden of
proof is almost always on the complainant and, especially in the
case of diseases, proof that the occupation was the sole cause is
difficult, especially if there is a time lag between the onset and visible
incidence of the disease as there is in cancer and certain lung diseases.
From time to time a union's legal department will be involved in test
cases involving diseases or injury and it is a signal victory if one is
successful. Recently, deafness was adjudged to be an 'industrial
injury' for the first time and this might open a flood-gate of similar
cases ranging from total deafness to varying degrees of partial
hearing. (This aspect of a union's work is treated in chapter nine.)

The 1971 Act and the learning process

The Industrial Relations Act created work for trade unions in a
legal setting which was an inevitability as that Act sought to bring
all collective bargaining into a legal framework. The two primary
agencies established were the Industrial Tribunals and the National
Industrial Relations Court (NIRC). The Tribunals were (and are)
based on areas. They are staffed by people living in that area and
consist of a chairman, generally having a legal background, and
two co-tribunal members. Oaths are taken, evidence given and
proceedings are based on normal court behaviour. The National
Industrial Relations Court sat in London and Glasgow. The President
of the Court, and his two co-chairmen, were High Court Judges and
the Court itself had the status of a High Court. The other members of
the Court were appointed by the Lord Chancellor's Office and sat,
as in the Tribunals, as side-men to the Chairman of the day. The
NIRC, although having a senior court status was far more informal
than the tribunals; no oath was administered, hearsay evidence was
allowed and robes were not worn.

But NIRC failed because it sought to redistribute power against
the flow of history. By and large the tribunals dealt with the less-
important cases or less important as defined by the drafters of the
Industrial Relations Act. Unfair dismissal cases and minor cases
under section 5 of that Act alleging discriminations were (and still
are) the staple fodder of the Tribunals. If a Tribunal came across a
case that it felt had an immediate national interest it could pass it
directly to the NIRC. All appeals from Tribunals went to NIRC,

all appeals from NIRC including appeals against judgment on appeals from Tribunals went to the Court of Appeal and appeals from that body were made to the House of Lords. Only one has yet been adjudicated upon at this highest level and that resulted in the interesting spectacle of a union appealing against an NIRC decision, the appeal court's upholding of the appeal being reversed by the House of Lords on appeal by the employer. One small, if bizarre, side-effect of the Court's existence was the emergence of the previously, almost totally, unknown figure of the Official Solicitor who, like a good fairy, popped out of the trap-door in the nick of time to save a national strike after the court had arranged for the gaoling of five trade unionists. The House of Lords decision now makes it far more difficult for such an imprisonment to take place.

Since then a new appellate Tribunal has been formed within the employee protection legislation; the Employment Appeal Tribunal.

Using the courts

Challenging government legislation when it is inimical to union policy and the well-being of its members is one such use of a union's legal department. The successful challenge to the Prices and Incomes Act in 1966 by ASTMS is an interesting example. In this case the union took employers to court to compel them to pay previously-negotiated increases to their employees. In one case the employer pleaded that legislation prevented him from doing so but the court ruled otherwise; a precedent was set and many ASTMS members protected their contractual rights. In the same area, but on a different and narrower point, USDAW took an employer (the Co-Op) to the County Court in 1973 and obtained a decision that some back pay should be paid when the employer was sheltering behind Phases I and II of the Counter Inflation Act. Both actions were legitimate tactical union uses of the judicial process.

A second use of the law is also in defence of members. The *News Chronicle* case mentioned in chapter seven is one example. Another recent example was over the transfer of the remaining 12 per cent of Chrysler shares left in Chrysler UK from British to Chrysler Corporation US ownership. ASTMS held ten shares valued at £1.40 in all and fought the case in the High Court as a shareholder. This introduces a tactic which, although not properly suited to this chapter, should be aired. A union can buy a token number of shares in the companies in which it has membership and this will entitle the union to have representatives at Annual General Meetings, and even nominate candidates for the board. This can be used to good effect as a statement describing bad industrial relations at a public company meeting cannot help that company with its existing or potential share-holders. In the Chrysler case although the company meeting was used the High Court needed to ratify the transfer of shares and, while there was some opposition of a commercial nature, ASTMS were alone in trying to defend its members amongst trade unions but in the event all the efforts failed and Chrysler became completely US owned. The subsequent consequences of this need not be under-lined.

Another use of the courts was an application for an injunction to stop pro-Common Market propaganda being paid for and distributed out of Government agency funds. This only failed on a technicality but succeeded to the extent it was widely publicised and a previously little-known decision had to stand in the full public gaze. The Government had to seek to justify its executive acts.

In the past, trade unions have taken a hammering at the hands of the legal processes and case law has been built up against them. From picketing prosecutions under strange old statutes through Rookes *v.* Barnard and the Industrial Relations Act collective bargaining and its methods have been circumscribed. Relationships between the unions and the law have been hard to decipher at times yet if used correctly the legal processes can be a useful adjunct to collective bargaining techniques.

Trade union officers are the professionals at industrial relations but often need to ally themselves with those who are the profes-sionals in legal matters. The Industrial Relations Act introduced the law into collective bargaining where it had earlier existed within a general case-law framework. A trade union, if it wishes to defend its members' interests (as they define them) must co-exist with the legal profession although the responsibility for the members' well-being must remain with the union and the full-time officials must adapt to all the new circumstances whenever they occur and whoever introduces them. At least one group of people in Britain can duly claim that 'All is love yet all is Law' and these are the lawyers who specialise in industrial relations.

Unfair dismissals

The concept of the 'Unfair dismissal' became established in British Law as a result of Section 12 of the 1971 Industrial Relations Act. When the Act was repealed in 1974 the Trade Unions and Labour Relations Act (the instrument of repeal) re-enacted these provisions. Some details such as qualifying working time and the time lag allowed before a case was judged were changed, but the basic principles remained the same. The Employment Protection Act later improved on these. Instead of compensation for loss of job being the basic remedy the emphasis changed to reinstatement or re-engagement with penalties for employers who refused to act on Tribunal orders involving additional awards to the aggrieved party.

The procedure is as follows: Any employee who alleges that his or her dismissal was unfair, and had been in continuous employment with that employer for six months or more, has three months to apply to an Industrial Tribunal for a declaration of unfairness and the consequent award. The Tribunal has the power to accept cases when more than three months have elapsed. The date of dismissal was earlier a subject for contention but it is now fixed as the termination of the employment. The Industrial Tribunal which hears, amongst other things, unfair dismissal cases, consists of a chairman who is legally qualified and two lay representatives, one nominated by the trade unions and the other from the employers.

A case cannot be heard by a Tribunal until a Conciliation Officer has had the opportunity to intervene and to try to settle the dispute. Only if this fails is the case heard. This does not mean that a complaint cannot be filed with the Tribunal and most often it is the Tribunal itself which contacts the Conciliation Officer.

The aggrieved employee has to make the initial complaint (and best on the advice of his or her trade union, although clearly many thousands are unrepresented and only eager to have their 'day in court'). Once the complaint has been made and the Secretary of the Tribunal has set a date for hearing, the trade union officer or appropriate union department is normally involved and notified of all the papers and proceedings.

A great deal of case law in Tribunal reports, old NIRC appeal cases and now High Court and EAT appeals has been built up on the details of what misbehaviour can be justified (on either side) in a dismissal case.

The basic reasons for unfair dismissal seem unchanged except in degree and detail. Dismissals are fair if they are on grounds of: (a) the capability or qualifications for the job involved being deficient; (b) the conduct of the employee warranted it; (c) redundancy; (d) continued employment would have contravened a law and (e) the 'catch all' of 'some other substantial reason'. Each of these can be argued in the Tribunal. What cannot be defended is the dismissal for 'inadmissible reasons'. These are dismissals for belonging to, intending to belong to, or taking action on behalf of an independent trade union as defined in the TULRA or refusing to join a non-independent trade union.

Constructive dismissal is also unfair but difficult to prove. This is where an employee is justified in leaving because of the employer's behaviour which has effectively robbed him of his job. An example would be a skilled technician being transferred to serve in a canteen against his will. A further reason is unfair selection for redundancy, generally on the grounds of independent trade union membership. Once a complaint has been brought with statements from the employee alleging that the dismissal was unfair the onus is on the employer to show that he had followed proper procedures including warnings and that the dismissal was for a fair reason.

Once the case has been submitted to the Tribunal, the Secretary of the Tribunals fixes a date for a hearing. The case is prepared by the aggrieved employee along with his local full-time official and the appropriate union department. The member can present the case himself or can use a full-time official, a solicitor, even a barrister. It is generally most advantageous to use a union official as it is a basic collective bargaining problem. Indeed, this type of case at the Tribunal is often only taken if other industrial relations reactions are inapplicable, for example the Ford strike in September 1973 over the dismissal of a TGWU member. However, it is hoped that the new Tribunal procedures will obviate the need for industrial action. The result follows the Tribunal hearing and can be either given immediately, or deferred, although there seem to be increasing delays in the rendering of decisions. If an unfair dismissal is found to have taken place the Tribunal has the power to order re-engagement or re-instatement (this itself could be in the form of a constructive dismissal) or award compensation.

At one time an entire section of employees missed the net of unfair dismissals. Those who were employed on fixed-term contracts which were initially for under two years' duration and latterly six months were excluded from the provisions. Those typically include research personnel picked for a specific project, university research assistants and associates, and consultancy staffs. This however has now changed as a result of both legislative action and case law.

The present situation is that the only exemptions from unfair dismissal are fixed-term contracts of under six months and over two years. The latter case is however qualified. There must be a specific exclusion clause written into the contract and there must be no period of notice. This latter point would mean that the contract was not fixed term but capable of being terminated within the stated term. In addition consecutive contracts count as one contract, for example, five, one-year, fixed-term contracts are construed as being a single, five-year contract. This package represents a step forward for what was a disadvantaged class of employee. Of course the case has to be proved, and this is often very difficult but at least it can now be taken.

Before the Employment Protection Act, reinstatements and re-engagements were rare and the compensatory payments, although theoretically up to a maximum of £5,400 were normally very low. This has now changed. Anyone who has been unfairly dismissed gets a minimum of two weeks' pay and this runs up on the age, length of service, redundancy-payments scale. If reinstatement or re-engagement is not ordered (it is no longer a recommendation) a compensatory payment of up to £5,400 may be awarded by the Tribunal. Finally, if the Tribunal's award of reinstatement or re-engagement is not acted upon penalty payments of between twenty-six and fifty-two weeks at a maximum of £80 per week can be made to the dismissed employee. However it is the duty of the employee to mitigate his or her loss and compensatory payments are often reduced for failure to do so. This is generally construed as attempts to find alternative employment, successfully or otherwise.

Appeals on points of law can be made to the Employment Appeal Tribunal (EAT) set up under the Employment Protection Act and having the status of a High Court.

Early in the cases of unfair dismissal a new concept was finally realised, that of 'property in jobs'. New is perhaps the wrong adjective, as property in a job is a medieval concept which hitherto had been applied solely to the types of employment such as clergymen of the Church of England, Judges and Field Marshals. When there is property in a job dismissal cannot be valid unless a judicial enquiry is held at which the threatened employee is allowed to present his case. Legal research by ASTMS asserts that the wording of the Act confers property in all jobs in Britain. If legal precedents are followed, any dismissals which have taken place since the implementation of the Industrial Relations Act should be null and void and the technical reinstatement should include back pay to the time of dismissal. The concept has not yet been tested. Since the enactment of the unfair-dismissal procedures and their subsequent amendments many people have had awards made to them. If the awards, in themselves, have not deterred employers from un-justified dismissals the effect and often the publicity involved have had a cautionary effect. The procedures have, to a marked extent, given a more secure future for all of those who must enter the labour market.

Chapter 7

Redundancies

'Must you go, can't you stay' – Charles John Vaughan

Causes

Redundancies, like motor accidents, are things that happen to other people. They should not be confused with dismissals which, as we have seen, are dealt with by trade unions under a grievance procedure. Technically an employee is not redundant, the job is redundant and it no longer exists to be filled by another worker. The insecurity within the British labour force, be they shop floor sweepers or executive directors, is in large part due to this newish development and its rapid extension. Technological redundancies were once considered to be an all-pervasive and dreadful evil. The Luddites smashed machinery in the belief that it would, if left to operate, create huge reservoirs of unemployment, the new concept of technological unemployment. Each new advance in technology which goes to create a more capital intensive – and less labour intensive – process does have some redundancy effects but it also has other features. The motor-car industry would not have boomed had it not been for capital intensive techniques cutting long term unit costs and thus making vehicles available to a wider range of income groups. The same argument applies to petroleum-refining plants, the use of plastics and the new and large variety of processes and materials which have resulted in fewer employees per unit of output. In all these cases the goods or service has become available to more people thus, supposedly, improving their standard of living. Another reason for redundancies is the running down of an old industry. In a sense this is merely the technological argument restated and the examples of coal mining, railways and cotton spinning in Britain are clear enough. The railways have been truncated partly out of political dogmatism and jaundiced accountancy but partly because, in some areas, demand for the services had fallen due to car ownership. From 1960 the number of British Rail employees fell from 509,848 to 257,010 in 1970 or a loss of 49·6 per cent of the labour force over the decade. The coal mining industry has been contracting for many years with unprofitable, or marginally profitable, pits being closed in the belief that other fossil fuels and perhaps nuclear power would prove to be the energy providers of the future. The Lancashire cotton industry has contracted in the face of overseas competition and the technological advances made in man-made fibres. In each case the work force has been drastically cut but overall (except in small mining communities) it has been relatively painless.

A third reason for redundancies is commercial viability in the private and public sectors. The Rolls-Royce management fiasco resulted in many lost jobs, the BSA failure cost 3,000 posts and the British Steel closures in Wales and Scotland created immense local job problems. Commercial success is measured in many ways but one commonly used yardstick is 'satisfying' (comparing the performance with that of another enterprise but using imperfect information) and in this, as in other criteria, the cost or profitability in social terms is not recognised. Take-overs are an extension of this redundancy-causing situation. The classic reason for a genuine take-over was the creation of economies of scale in a larger unit subsequently and charmingly phrased as 'industrial synergy'. A prime British exponent of this method has been Sir Arnold Weinstock and his gigantic General Electric Company complex. The merging of GEC, AEI, Elliots, Marconi and others has not gone happily for the employees of the concerns. The Woolwich plant closure and consequent redundancies were the first in a wave of such re-organisations. The effect on the employees has been catastrophic in terms of personal stress – and for those left in the factories uncertainty as to where the axe will fall next has been a great tension builder.

Government measures can cause redundancies either deliberately or as an accidental spin-off from policies designed to deal with other problems. The imposition of the Selective Employment Tax was a deliberate attempt to make employment in the manufacturing sector relatively cheaper to an employer than in the service sector. The policy was to increase national productive capacity by releasing labour (part of which had an almost zero marginal product) from service industries. It failed and, in the long term, it seems clear that the strategy was none other than grossly harmful. In 1971 the Government correctly diagnosed their problem as inflation; it then incorrectly diagnosed it as cost-push inflation and managed to refine their mis-diagnosis even further by inventing the new economic concept of wage-push inflation. Traditional economic theory has always suggested that this form of inflation can be cured by un-employment, by creating a job market with surplus labour. The Phillips Curve, at the time beloved of the Treasury, even explained how to achieve a desired reduction in the rate of inflation in quantita-tive terms. The resulting 'lame duck' philosophy and hard credit policies eventually put 1.5 million people out of work. The rate of inflation slowed but not that much and at an immense long term cost to the British asset base. An adjunct to this is the current pre-occupation with public spending and, obviously, cuts in this not only create unemployment in the public sector, but also in the sup-plying industries in the private sector.

Asset stripping has also been a great redundancy maker. Asset stripping was practised quietly for years by the conglomerate founders but it took a series of highly publicised ventures by entrepreneurs such as Mr John Bentley and his Barclay Securities for the truth to be publicly illuminated. The method is simplicity itself: find a smallish company on hard times, low earnings, preferably with liquidity problems but with large fixed assets. Then take it over using money from other conglomerates, your own company or, as some have done in the past, money taken from the company to be taken over – then or later. Then re-organise the company. This entails the selling of all readily realisable assets which are not profitable as means of production i.e., land, freeholds and leases of property, machines, etc. The revenue then enables a speculator to purchase a slightly larger company next time around. Meanwhile, the original employees have seen their jobs gone and their company either truncated beyond all belief or wound up stripped of all its assets.

There are thus many reasons leading to redundancies including withdrawal of Government funds from research projects and establishment; the re-organisation of Local Government and the National Health Service or the withdrawal of a multi-national company. In most cases the argument used by management is improved efficiency and progress, and the safe-guarding of the jobs of others. Executives and management are not fire-proof from this phenomenon. The age of management consultancy and optimisa-tion of all resources is upon us and senior executives are as vulnerable as anyone. When ASTMS ran an advertisement in the national press, 'The Board and I do not like the colour of your eyes', the response was overwhelming, the managers' personal identification with the crisis was striking.

Trade unions cannot sit by and let members be put out of work. Although some people feel that the Protestant ethic has penetrated too deeply into the trade union movement and the slogan 'The

Right to Work' should be replaced by the more hedonist 'Right to Leisure', a capitalist society, such as Britain, is built upon expectations. These expectations and goals can only be achieved by the spending of money on goods and services. In depriving a man or woman of their right to participate in this free for all by removing the means of entry one is depriving them of their position and justification for themselves in society.

If it is not possible for a trade union to stop all of, some of, or postpone, the redundancies it can make one point quite firmly. It is that its members will leave through a money-shaped exit. There are many arguments, tactics and procedures in a trade union's armoury on this issue and we will list them. First, it would be as well to sketch in the present statutory situation affecting redundancies.

Redundancy Payments Act

The Redundancy Payments Act was enacted in 1965 and has subsequently been amended eight times. It provides for a fund which is made up of employer and government contributions. Each employer pays weekly, or monthly, into the fund amounts which are related to the number of his employees. In a redundancy situation money is paid from the fund, which is a national one and the Government pay their share. The benefits are paid according to the length of continuous service with the company and the age of the employee. Benefits were last fixed in July 1975 and since then to the date of writing the Pound has depreciated in value by 5·4 per cent so that, in real terms, statutory redundancy benefits are far from generous, especially as the maximum allowable payment is thirty weeks × £80 = £2,400 or, in real terms as of February 1976 £2,270. Other considerations such as likelihood of further employment and regional variations ought to be, but are not, taken into account and this has become, once again, one of the prime responsibilities of a trade union. But there is now a statutory fall-back position for those displaced. The trade union function is to initially try to prevent redundancies, then minimise them and finally to make sure that the Redundancy Payments Act compensation is treated as a minimum entitlement. One small point on the Redundancy Payments situation shows how unsatisfactory it can be. Employees within ten years of retirement date and eligible for a company pension have their compensation reduced to take the pension into account yet it is precisely these men and women of fifty-five who are unlikely to find alternative employment and need more money than some other categories.

Pre-emptive agreements

A trade union can try to pre-empt a redundancy situation by negotiating a redundancy agreement with management at a time when no such problems exist or are even in the wind. This has a slight disadvantage in that it can sow seeds of doubt as to the future of the employees as well as the employer. This is not over-serious as there is a fundamental point to be taken into account. In a capitalist society there has, so far, been no right to work. Capitalism works on an accountancy profit motive, if redundancies or indeed unemployment of a structural type is essential to this profit then, unless the system changes the employee must be at the mercy of those controlling the capital. A right to work implies that society itself will provide work if all else fails, but only the Government can do this and if it is in a position to do so it will not be a truly capitalist society. Keynsian deficit budgeting and public works commitments are a reaction to situations where people are out of work and as we have shown, Governments may prefer not to use them as shown in 1971 or 1975.

A pre-redundancy agreement will start in the same fashion as a procedure agreement in defining the moves of the parties and the categories of workers to be considered in the agreement. There will be a clause to the effect that any employee who becomes subject to the agreement will do so only after consultations between the parties to the agreement and after every effort has been made by both sides to prevent it happening. There may be a procedural timetable for these discussions. The first stage might be notification of any redundancy plans by the management to the union at least sixteen weeks before the date on which redundancies will start. Negotiations take place during this period up to national official level if necessary.

If some employees have to go it is essential that as long a period of notice before the issuing of redundancy notices is given, as well as adequate compensation, in order to allow the employees the maximum time to arrange for suitable alternative employment – if possible and if they are at the right age. The agreement may also lay down the ground rules as to who will leave should there be a partial redundancy. The most common method of selection in Britain is on the LIFO principle, i.e. 'last in, first out'. This is dependent on the departments in which the run down will take place and should not normally be a plant-wise LIFO. This system has been found to be the most equitable and, most importantly, is seen to be equitable by the whole of the employees involved. It can be assumed that in any given situation those who have worked for a company the longest will have put down the deepest roots and thus have the most to lose. There can of course be exceptions to this rule; marital status, number of children, children's schools, disabilities and physical handicaps are just some of the extenuating circumstances which can and should force a revision of a formal schedule. It is important that these changes emanate from, and are settled by, the trade union side. If the management side attempts to 'buck the system' it will inevitably be suspected of keeping its own blue-eyed boys and victimising union members or activists. The agreement must then lay down the conditions under which employees will leave. There is often a table based on the Redundancy Payment Act but amended to negotiated compensation-payment levels. An alternative is to have the compensation on a straight-line basis, dependent on the years worked e.g., one month's salary for each continuous year's service with the employer up to certain maxima. The Inland Revenue authorities allow redundancy payments, or severance pay, of up to £5,000 on a tax-free basis, while sums above this are taxed at earned-income rate. The table of Redundancy Payments reaches a peak at ages sixty-two to sixty-five because of the nearness to retirement. Ideally one would like to construct a table taking into account the occupational pension that the redundant employee will receive, bringing it to a present value and arranging for equitability in this manner. Unfortunately, so many employees in Britain either have no occupational scheme or receive a disgracefully low one that other than for some non-manual staff employees, it is basically an academic exercise in many cases.

Legislation and minimum standards

The Employment Protection Act improves the warning that employees will be able to get. Redundancy situations where more than 100 employees are involved require advance consultations with the recognised independent unions at least ninety days before the first of the dismissals take effect and, in the case of between ten and ninety-nine employees, thirty-days notice will have to be given. Consultations are expected to start with written statements by the employer outlining the reasons, the numbers affected and methods proposed for selection and dismissal. A similar notice has also to be sent to the Secretary of State for Employment. If an employer does not comply with these provisions the union can complain to an Industrial Tribunal which may in turn issue what will be known as a 'Protective Award'. This would mean payment by the company to all the dismissed employees for a period not exceeding ninety days and alongside of this there may be a reduction in the rebate due to an employer from the Redundancy Payments Fund. It seems unlikely that the provision on consultations will be ignored by management except as an oversight.

Although such improvements are welcome in that they set new and desirable minimum standards of conduct, they do not really come to terms with the problem. A decently-managed society needs to be able, and should be able, to smooth the path for those made redundant by both a monetary compensation and the provision of a new job. The Manpower Services Commission, although representing a step in the right direction has neither the resources nor the legislative backing to provide a labour market planning mechanism approaching, say, the Swedish level. The Labour Market Board in Sweden can not only compel very early notification of redundancy and dismissals but also has powers to direct investment into areas where the redundancies are taking place. The training and re-training provisions available in Sweden can accept 3 per cent of their labour force at any one time and the courses run the gamut of skills and academic subjects – including foreign-language degrees. In Britain we traditionally retrain or train people to be carpenters, bricklayers, lathe operators and other traditional tradesmen. What we need is technologically-oriented skill and training combined with a radical reappraisal of what both individuals and our society need.

Pensions and redundancy

This leads directly into the question what is the role of pension schemes in a redundancy situation? The Inland Revenue authorities now allow early-retirement pensions to be paid at age fifty (a relaxation of the previous rule permitting payment only within ten years of normal retirement). Many redundant employees are over fifty and, occasionally, schemes cater for 'early retirement at the company's behest' and generally the pension is payable immediately without an actuarial reduction, or it can be preserved, or transferred to a new employer. The 'wipe out' reduction clause is important and can mean a large increase in pension for a man of fifty whose reduction would be inordinate (that is, large enough to wipe out 60 per cent of his pension). The actuarial reduction is based on the premise that the pension has to be paid over a longer period and the employee has contributed less because of fewer years worked. The redundancy compensation is, of course, paid in addition to the company pension provisions. There is no reason why an employee pensioned in this way cannot take another job; the only penalty is a large tax bill. These then are the pre-emptive ploys. The other method is to wait for redundancies to be mooted and at that point in time to negotiate with the company. Why should there be compensation paid to a redundant employee at all? Legally there is no obligation for an employer to do anything in excess of the Redundancy Payments Act and the pension fund trust deed – should one exist.

When the *News Chronicle* owners decided to give up in 1960 the management decided to pay enhanced redundancy compensation. The shareholders of the company successfully took legal action to prevent the management disposing of their assets in this way, on the grounds that the directors' responsibility was solely to the share-holders. This may change but, meantime it can be difficult to pay enhanced compensation in a wind-up situation.

Future prospects

When an employee loses a job there is first shock, second unemploy-ment, and third the realisation that although the salary has gone, the commitments remain. Mortgage repayments or rent, rates, food, clothing, hire purchase repayments on cars and consumer durables go on. If the person is unfortunate enough to live in a high-structural unemployment area there is the long-term problem of trying to find a job near existing housing and schools. The economists always mutter that mobility of labour is low in Britain. But the problem is severe and many sided. If the employee owns his own house, who will buy it in a depressed area if there have been large-scale redundancies? If a buyer is found it is often at below the original buying price and this inhibits a family moving to any new area. If the ex-employee lives in municipal dwellings any move to a fresh location will put him at the bottom of the council waiting list so that an area 'tied cottage' exists and money is needed to ease and lubricate his movement. A family will need money to travel to see new accommodation, view new schools, purchase new school uniforms, furniture and the thousand and one things needed for a decent quality of life.

All these issues are separate from the claim that redundancy payments are an employee's right based on his property rights in his job. 'Golden handshakes' in the post-Second World War situation established this property right at senior executive and board levels but a more junior employee can only sell his or her skills and labour and, if not on a fixed term contract, expects the contract to be honoured in the indefinite term. A redundancy is a unilateral breaking of the contract and as the employer must have made a profit out of the employee during his working life and the redundancy is to aid future corporate profits it is reasonable to expect the employer to incur a penalty.

Union negotiations

There are many tactical reasons for delaying the negotiation of redundancy settlements to the time when redundancies are announced. The employees will then work in a highly-charged atmosphere and will be more militant or at least the employer *thinks* they will be more militant. The more closed and tight the community the higher the degree of militancy. The second point is publicity. In general, British employers are sensitive to adverse publicity and what can be worse than putting elderly men and women with years of service onto the dole queue without as much as a gold watch? For some unaccountable reason British employers still care to foster the impression that they are not in business to make profits but as a service first to the public, and second to the nation. The main reason that 'asset stripping' became such a dirty phrase was the ruthlessly clumsy way in which it was done, and the publicity about the consequent unemployment. Yet the men responsible, instead of keeping a low profile, went out of their way to explain their motives and to justify their own actions, thereby bringing the whole matter more clearly into the public consciousness.

Local pressures on a trade union headquarters are at their heaviest in a redundancy situation. This should surprise no-one. Members join a trade union for protection, they join that union at their place of work and not in an abstract situation; a redundancy threat is a primal threat. In circumstances such as these trade unions have to pull out all the stops. The first job is to prevent any redundancies. Union officials will meet the management at local level to discuss the situation and to determine the reasons for and the scale of the proposed dismissals. The reasons can be any of the ones mentioned earlier. The scale can vary too. Departments can be closed and this especially applies to research and development areas which are often the first to go in a general economic or trade recession. It may be a general 'shake-out' or 'head-count' to cut the salary bill by an inefficient employer or it may be 'genuine' disaster involving the total closure of the plant or liquidation of the company.

The exploratory meetings are followed by negotiating meetings, sometimes at local and sometimes at national level where the aim is always to prevent or minimise redundancies. It may appear obvious that to save the company some redundancies will have to be made; it may appear inevitable that the enterprise might have to go into liquidation. At times such as these trade unions use reasonable arguments, persuasion, pressures and intense lobbying. In a limited redundancy situation there are the normal industrial sanctions that

can be applied and, more and more frequently, the imposition of a
'sit-in' or a refusal to leave the company's facilities. In a total
closure situation, the famous 'work-in' at the Upper Clyde and the
sit-ins at the Plessey plant at Alexandria and other sites have
proved most effective. It is notable that unprofitable enterprises
have become potentially workable when action of this type is taken
and especially when equipment cannot be sold off. The normal
sanctions run from non-co-operation through to an indefinite strike.
A redundancy situation is one which although potentially divisive
usually creates a unity within the workforce.

Sit-ins and work-ins

It is worth treating the sit-ins and work-ins in slightly more detail
as they are relatively recent on the industrial relations scene. They
are significant in that capitalism is still about property and this is a
method of temporarily detaining the assets in the system. The Upper
Clyde ship-builders occupation was a work-in and not to be confused
with a sit-in. Other notable work-ins were at Briant Colour-Printers
in 1972, the French, Lip watch factory in 1973 and the work-in at
Norton Villiers Triumph in 1975. In all cases *some* jobs have been
preserved by the tactic, although not necessarily under the same
employer. At Upper Clyde the workers defied local management
and the Heath Government's 'lame duck' policy and established that
the yards had commercial viability. It was the workers' leaders and
trade unions who solicited and finally clinched the deal with the
US-based Marathon Company. Had this action not been taken a
massive redundancy in an already high unemployment area was
inevitable. One reason for the success was that, although it is easy
to brand a withdrawal of labour as disruptive, it was hard similarly
to categorise a refusal to stop work. The major point made was that
both the management and the Government were incompetent as the
workers were the only ones who appreciated the potential of the
yards and subsequently proved they could manage them and
conduct business negotiations. A national asset was thus preserved
on the Clyde. The sit-in is different, it is an occupation designed to
preserve access to the department or whole plant. It is effective in
cases where an asset stripper wishes to get at machinery to sell but
cannot, or where a computer block is occupied and the computer is
needed for invoices and wages in a classic high-profile case. In the
first instance there has been a total closure of plant, in the second
redundancies have been in a specific department. The sit-in at an
empty plant is generally born out of desperation when all else has
failed; it is embarrassing to the former owners and indeed decisions

have changed and plants stayed open because of it as in Courtaulds at Skelmersdale in 1972.

Preventive measures

Other tactics can be tried in a collective bargaining sense. One sensible method is to negotiate a 'no involuntary redundancy' agreement as was done at the Prudential Assurance Company on the well tried basis that prevention and therapy is better than crisis. The result of this is that if the company wishes to cut their labour force it must be done either by halting recruitment or operating a voluntary, early retirement scheme. A second method is jointly to agree to a rundown by managing the natural wastage in the labour force that is normal in any industrial or commercial enterprise. That is, not to replace staff who leave, and to cut down on recruitment; a method used extensively by British Rail. Care must be taken however that a smaller labour force is not intended to do the same work as the larger one without commensurate increases in remuneration. Another tactic is to negotiate an agreement which promises to re-employ those who wish to be re-employed with the same employer but at a different plant. The National Coal Board have used this system. A corollary of this is compensation based on unemployment time. The agreement will stipulate that £X will be paid as compensation but that if the ex-employee is still unemployed after three months an additional sum is paid and again after six, nine and twelve months. There were 'rescue' clauses of this type in the agreement with GEC over the closure of the old AEI Woolwich plant.

Early retirement schemes as in the insurance industry are the subject of straight collective bargaining between unions and management. The first point to establish is that it is voluntary; second that as it is in the interest of the employer, the employee will have to be induced to go by being offered sufficiently attractive terms. Early retirement must imply a pension payment and the negotiations therefore usually centre around the pension scheme plus a lump-sum compensation. Where possible, the pension should be enhanced by the addition of added years of service, not merely actuarially unreduced, and the lump sum should represent compensation for a loss of salary and the inevitable difficulties facing, for example, a fifty-eight-year old insurance worker seeking another job. If fringe benefits were previously enjoyed (such as low-interest house mortgages) then these must also be protected. The re-organisation of the Health Service and Local Government resulted in the duplication of some posts, especially in administrative positions and this has been recognised by a generous early retirement scheme with enhanced pensions. Although pensions can have added years of benefit built-in, the rules of the scheme are inviolate. Typically, at the Prudential Assurance Company the pension was based on the average of the last three years' salary. To bring this to an acceptable level of remuneration at the time of retirement an additional lump sum was negotiated which, if invested in an annuity, would bring the pension up to the required standard. The following year and, influenced by these negotiations, the Prudential pension scheme was re-negotiated and pensionable salary was re-defined as the final year's salary. One advantage to a company of an early retirement scheme is that it opens its promotion channels by creating slots for the younger members of staff to be promoted, thus both stimulating interest in the company and helping the company retain its career-oriented employees. This incentive for management gives extra leverage to the union in the creation of improved conditions.

Lobbying and a case study

Collective bargaining is not exclusively a process for settling issues between employers and trade unions for both sides make use of contacts in Parliament, federations and the mass media. Nowhere in the field of industrial relations are these extensions more important than in potential or actual redundancy situations. In general terms a well organised trade-union will attempt to enlist the aid of MPs, either its own members or the member in whose constituency the redundancies would occur. This can take place in two distinct stages, for example, before anything has happened in a pre-emptive exercise or after the first announcements in a reactive way. The decisions to continue production of the Concorde provide a good example of the first case. There has been much discussion about the financial burdens imposed by Concorde and its lack of commercial viability reflected in the dropping of options by airlines and the lack of definite sales. If Concorde were to be axed, over 10,000 workers, directly or indirectly, would be affected by loss of employment in the very first stages. There is a vocal anti-Concorde lobby but in a more effective way trade unions have been telling the Government their feelings on possible unemployment resulting from cancellation of the project. A joint committee of French–British trade unions was created and has repeatedly lobbied French and British company officials, ministers and MPs to make their views known and mount a trans-national union approach to the subject. This lobbying was the effective, counter pressure; Concorde is still a viable project and work is continuing. An individual union can do a lot in this sphere if it has a well defined and working Parliamentary presence. The benefit of a well thought programme for sponsoring and briefing MPs then becomes very clear.

A good example of the amount of work that has to go into a major redundancy is the Rolls-Royce collapse in 1971. When the Government announced that the company was going into receivership, no redundancies had been announced but the trouble was diagnosed as faulty pricing techniques for the RB211 engines to be fitted to the Lockheed Tristar. The Government announced it would take parts of Rolls-Royce into ownership and unilaterally renege on the contract with Lockheed, almost precipitating the collapse of that company in turn. Once again we find impending redundancies due to faulty management (and informative auditing systems over many years) combined with unilateral and philosophically motivated Government action. The employees suffer and the trade unions have to pick up the pieces. When the new board of Rolls-Royce 1971 was appointed a massive redundancy was announced affecting both the Derby and East Kilbride complex. Derby *is* Rolls-Royce. The company dominated the town physically and for employees the position was shattering for employment. Rolls-Royce had been classed with the Bank of England as the paragon of safety and the hallmark of British technical and engineering excellence and superiority throughout the world. This 'institutionalised' concept permeated the consciousness of employees so the crash became that much harder to take and bewilderment and trauma took the place of militancy in some instances. The aero-engine division was the one cut back most severely; this division employed more technical specialists than any other and thus the chances of suitable alternative employment elsewhere were remote. The fear reflected itself in sudden withdrawals from the Derby Building Society which was reminiscent of the 1930s. From the outset the nation and the employees were stunned but it was equally obvious that unless something drastic was done the RB211 project as a world leader in a new generation of jet engines with environmental advantages would be cancelled and Derby reduced to ghost-town status with Bristol and the Scottish complex of factories reduced to disaster-area status. Whether redundancies were needed except as a justification of government policy is a debatable point but predictably they came. The employees suffered in three ways; by loss of jobs earnings and purchasing power plus loss of value in property and loss of savings. Many employees had their savings invested in the Rolls-Royce Workers share scheme and as unsecured, non-preferred creditors their chances of recovery of substantial monies looked slim. (In fact in 1973 after valiant work by the

Receiver and others all Worker Shares surprisingly were redeemed in full.)

The unions were thus faced with several discrete problems. They had to minimise the redundancies, arrange for adequate compensation, try to obtain full payment for Workers Shares, and also safeguard the future of Rolls-Royce 1971 and the hived-off subsidiaries. Redundancy payments were negotiated and were not unreasonable. The pension funds were analysed and found to be safeguarded (not always the case) if slightly depleted. A lot of work was done to try to find methods of redeeming Worker Shares and finally, as stated, the Receiver, after many representations, cajoled the creditors into paying the value in full. Protection of the future of the RB211 and safeguarding the future of Rolls-Royce 1971 (and thus minimising redundancies) was more complex and involved the use of extra-traditional union activities. At ASTMS the national officers had a technical crash course into the details of Titanium hollow core rotor blades, Hyfil leading edges and jet exhaust systems. Press conferences were held and the media widely covered them on the viability and desirability of the engine. Officers and MPs met the appropriate ministers, briefed other MPs with constituency interest in the matter. As there was a general postal workers' strike the general secretary of ASTMS flew to Washington, New York and Los Angeles to discuss the matter with American trade union officials and Lockheed company executives carrying a suitcase of letters for every member of the House of Representatives and the US Senate urging a rescue of Lockheed with a special representation to the chairmen of key Senate and House committees. The project was saved by one Senate vote, jobs were saved, the cost of the union's effort was high and in terms of other work foregone equally high but if jobs are at risk the union must always be ready to mobilise.

Other matters

As a tool for the future the union then commissioned a sociological survey to find out exactly what happened to all the technicians and managerial staffs who were made redundant. We summarise these findings, as some of these results were extremely interesting. Samples were taken of the 4,300 employees whose dismissals were announced in March 1971. It was found that 10 per cent found jobs immediately, 53 per cent were employed within three months and 74 per cent were re-employed by February 1972 leaving 26 per cent skilled, highly qualified employees out of a job eleven months after the dismissals had taken place. Of this last group almost 40 per cent were still actively trying to find employment whilst 46 per cent were retraining. Almost all the men seeking work were in their fifties or sixties. In these cases the Government agencies concerned could not cope with the problems. When a company liquidation is the cause of the redundancies great care and expertise must be exerted to check that the pension funds are secure and intact. A self-funded scheme may have a large percentage of its funds invested in its own equity or property. If this is the case the funds will take their place amongst the other creditors and may not be able to meet the present and future demands. This is especially true at that moment in time because of the immediate amounts of cash which have to be paid out.

There is also the case of a management which does not pay either its contributions into the fund, the members' contributions into the fund, or both. One or other of these situations was found when Beagle Aircraft and Eagle International went into liquidation and when Sexton Sons and Everard folded. There have been other cases of what Receivers have termed 'administrative inadvertence'. In these cases the union must register the fund members as preferential creditors with the Receiver; in all winding-up cases the Receiver and Liquidator become prime targets for union representations. Unpaid wages of up to four months, holiday pay, etc., must be claimed from the Liquidator; other similar savings or health scheme funds have to be claimed from the Receiver.

The Employment Protection Act will, however, alter this state of affairs. Arrears in pay of up to eight weeks, notice payments, holiday payments, but not pension fund payments in general, may be made payable from the Redundancy Payments Fund. An application for this to happen must be made to the Secretary of State for Employment. This removes the problem of competing with trade creditors and shareholders for what are often extremely limited amounts of money. Thus a substantial move is made towards guaranteeing payment for work that has been done.

Payments of pension contributions either collected from the employees or from the employer on behalf of employees which had not reached the pension fund as of the date of insolvency may also be paid from the Redundancy Payments Fund into the pension fund. A case such as this arose when Sexton Sons and Everard went into liquidation and under the trust deed and existing law there was nothing the former employees could do to make good their loss in spite of the most detailed researches by their union.

Redundancies or the threat of redundancies feature importantly in the trade unions' protective collective bargaining work. The tactics outlined above, even of the Press Conference and vigorous publicity, succeed far better than an individual seeking to do the same things. This is due to the leverage that a trade union has; it stands for a collective membership, it stands for a derived body of opinion rather than a single opinion and, as such, the impact of these initiatives is that much greater. Any trade union which takes a pride in its professionalism must explore all the avenues mentioned above. Above all it must try to monitor what is happening in the public and private sectors of industry, monitor the take-over scene, perhaps even make representations to the Monopolies Commission as ASTMS did in the Beechams, Boots, Glaxo take-over triangle in 1971 – and all to prevent redundancies. If one employee is prevented from being made redundant by these methods the money and resources spent on the exercise will have been worthwhile.

Chapter 8

Pensions

'*Old Age a Regret*' – Disraeli

Deferred income

The groundswell of feeling amongst trade union members on the subject of pensions is now marked and presages a new approach to the subject. The current interest stems from three distinct phenomena: the uncertainty and lack of confidence created by the unemployment in 1972, the dangers of the frozen 1.5 million out of work in 1976 and the pace of structural change. In addition the large and complicated 'Social Security Act' followed by the Social Security Pensions Act, although imperfectly understood, has impinged on people's consciousness and stimulated some thought on pensions schemes. The TUC has aided this movement with a detailed booklet on the latest pension arrangements and advice for trade unions on how to cope with the technicalities involved.

In many senses the British trade union movement arrived very late on the scene as far as pensions are concerned, with only the central and local government and other white-collar unions taking much active interest prior to 1972. This is surprising when one considers that a good scheme costs at least 18 per cent of payroll to fund and, assuming that the costs are split in a two to one ratio between employer and employee, this represents a continuing 12 per cent payroll liability to an employer which, in anyone's currency, is a lot of money.

Pensions should be looked upon as deferred incomes which indeed they are. A company not only pays salaries but provides a whole host of elements each of which contributes to the salary package. This package represents the remuneration which an employer must pay to recruit and retain his workers and staff but it also has a distinct social implication. A pension scheme is an integral part of this package. It can be thought of as a future payment for the use of the employee's time and skills whilst, in addition, acknowledging the part the employee has played in creating the wealth of the enterprise. Employers have now much more frequently to provide good pension schemes to recruit staff. A brief look at advertisements for jobs will show the importance of pensions as an invitation to change jobs and in modern times of labour mobility an employer has to be 'up market', particularly in city-centre situations. One reason for the attractiveness of pension schemes for workers is the appallingly low standard of state provisions and the apparent willingness of the electorate to allow such widespread deprivation. Another reason is that the social ethos in Britain does not embrace the 'extended family' concept and the taking in of the aged by the family unit as in Eastern and African cultures. People become justifiably uneasy and lonely after retirement and an adequate pension becomes the only means of retaining both self-respect and adequate living standards.

Viewed in this light, occupational pension schemes cease to be the eccentric charity of an odd radical employer but a payment to be had, as of right. This accepted, the logical conclusion is to negotiate the pension scheme; it seems easy but in practice is most complicated.

Legislative changes

Complications come in all degrees and sizes. First, legislation in the shape of the Social Security Pensions Act impinges; then the 1970 Finance Act; a plethora of Inland Revenue regulations; and finally the actuaries. Life is made even more difficult by the fact that, generally, the management side still has little idea of what is allowable and negotiations are adjourned for hours whilst actuaries are consulted. At a recent series of negotiations with a major employer there were three adjournments – each in excess of four hours.

There has been no settled background against which to negotiate pensions since 1970 when the Crossman plan fell along with the Labour Government. The Social Security Act which then filled a vacuum was not due for implementation until April 1975, but in February 1974 that Government fell and along with it the new legislation. The Social Security Pensions Act was then enacted and in itself was radically different to either of the previous legislative attempts. Some measures, however, such as the Occupational Pensions Board and the regulations regarding the preservation of pension entitlements were carried over from the previous Act. The new Act is not due for implementation until 1978, but some of the provisions will be brought in (or have already been implemented) at an earlier date.

At present there is a flat-rate retirement pension financed out of earnings-related contributions up to a cut-off point of one and three quarters times national average earnings. The previous earnings-related 'top-up' scheme has been frozen and the benefits will be inflation proofed. The only other existing retirement provisions are occupational schemes linked to employment.

The new arrangements

As of 1978 these provisions will change with the addition of a government earnings-related, second-tier scheme. In turn this scheme will set the minimum standards for all occupational schemes. Employers will be able to contract their employees into or out of the second-tier scheme but only after discussions with the appropriate unions and thus trade unions will be forced, whether or not they wish it, to be involved in occupational pension matters.

The second-tier scheme has far higher benefit provisions than the Tories proposed in their State Reserve Scheme and it embodies a far greater degree of equality in respect of men and women. For an employee contracted into the State Scheme the pension will be based on an accrual rate of 1/80 of pensionable salary per year of service, the scheme maturing after twenty years. Pensionable salary is worked out on an uprated twenty-year basis, that is to say that pensionable salary is the average of the last twenty years' salaries each of which has been given a present-day value using the Retail Price Index. There will be widows pensions, chronic ill-health pensions and inflation-proofing. All registered occupational schemes must be at least as good as the second-tier schemes and must also be required to show that the funds are capable of providing these benefits. However these conditions only apply to a scheme for benefits up to the minimum pension (second tier) standard. Most schemes in the white-collar sector are based on accrual rates of 1/60 and these will not have to 'guarantee' benefits over the 1/80 level, or on the other benefits conditional upon this advantage.

Contracting in or out

In the past (indeed at the time of writing) unions have negotiated pension schemes with an employer knowing that the only alternative was the basic, state scheme. In the near future the first decision to be taken will be whether to contract in or out of the second-tier scheme. Some unions have been advised to contract in and it is likely that many employers will be only too pleased to accept. The cost of providing an occupational scheme to meet the standards required will probably be greater than that incurred by contracting in and the insurance companies are fearing a large loss in their pension business. Certainly some manual workers with, for the most part, an historic disinterest in pension arrangements may permit this form of arrangement.

The white-collar sector with its traditional interest in pensions, reflected by the very superior staff schemes, will have to make one of the following choices. To contract out and have a full occupational scheme running alongside the basic state scheme even though this might prove to be expensive in practice, or to contract in and have a smaller scheme running on top of the second-tier scheme. Given the high historic level of the funds held and the prevailing ethos it is likely that this section of the work-force will contract out and 'carry on business as usual'. The rest of this chapter is based on this premise.

The preservation requirements carried over from the previous Act require some explanation. For years employers used the pension scheme as a 'tied-cottage benefit' by refusing either to transfer pensions to a new employer or preserve them until retirement date in the scheme. This meant that an employee who wished to change jobs could only withdraw his or her own contributions thus losing all the company contributions and also losing the pension entitlement – a considerable deterrent for (let us say) a forty-five-year old. The employer's contributions were retained in the fund and thus offset against future company contributions. The new legislation makes it compulsory for a scheme to preserve the pension of any employee who has worked for five or more continuous years for the company in question. As originally envisaged this was to be inflation proofed (as were all other pensions) at 3 per cent per year which in the light of recent economic history was tantamount to burning some of the money. Fortunately this has now changed and there is to be better inflation proofing up to minimum pension standard.

Multi-union negotiations

Pension schemes generally involve more than one union, often more than one company in a multi-plant situation and often many non-union members. The corollary of this is that pension negotiations in manufacturing industry are almost always conducted by a joint union panel. This can give an employer some possibility for attempting to divide the unions by emphasising differences they might have.

An example of this is where one union may have a preponderance of men who stay with the company for limited periods and then move on, whilst another might have most members who stay but whose early years with the company were spent on the shop floor in blue-collar jobs and thus have different pension entitlements for those years. The management could offer the stronger union what it requires, i.e., backfunding of past service thereby hoping that it will push for a settlement and relieve the company from instituting a proper, transferable system and saving money. To counter this the joint-union panel must settle on a policy overall and not depart from that policy. This had been done most effectively in the past in negotiations, although in one company twenty-three different unions have members in the pension scheme and to date no negotiations have taken place.

Actuaries

An Actuary's report on the old scheme (or schemes) is always useful but not essential. What is essential is a knowledge of the 1970 Finance Act and the Inland Revenue maxima. The discussion in a pension negotiation is as much about money as is any wage negotiation, but with one important difference. When negotiating wages, the present wage is known but quite often a management will not disclose how much money they put into a scheme, nor, except in overstated and rough terms how much more they intend to contribute. As each employee knows his or her contribution it is an unequal struggle. Given the fact that money is the key factor all the normal negotiating tactics are applicable, including industrial action, and this may be seen increasingly in the coming years. In July 1973 Britain's first major strike on pensions took place at the Dowty Rotol plant in Gloucester and involved 300 supervisors for two weeks. This is almost certainly the shape of things to come as union members realise the value and the vital necessity of occupational pension schemes.

It is interesting that the gas workers' dispute in early 1973 was settled when the pension scheme was adjusted and an actuarial surplus conjured out of thin air. It is equally interesting that at Dowty Rotol even the younger workers struck, against all predictions and indeed, company hopes.

What then, does one claim for in a pension scheme? A pension scheme is an inter-related package of benefits, few of which can be logically taken in isolation. If there are twenty on-cost elements in a scheme the available combinations of the elements is factorial twenty or $20 \times 19 \times 18 \ldots \times 2 \times 1$ – a rather large number.

Negotiating problems

In view of the complexities such a situation can bring to a negotiating table it may be that unions are negotiating pensions the wrong way. Pensions are about money. It should be possible to sit down with an employer and bargain for a global sum, for example 15 per cent of payroll and the division of this sum between the employer and the employees. Having done this the allocation of benefits can be made by a committee meeting in more amicable circumstances. This system would prevent a lot of the confusion which now arises out of details which more often than not works to the advantage of the employer. It may not be too long before such a negotiation is undertaken. However this is in the future and we now revert to the present.

Because of the inter-related nature of schemes it is important to get the basic elements of the scheme as good as possible as they repercuss on all the fringe benefits. The basics of a pension scheme are the definition of pensionable salary and how the pension accrues given the employees' years of service. These together give the prime pension.

Only one type of scheme, the final salary type, gives protection against inflation up to the time of retirement. Ideally one would like to see a pension based on the best year's salary in the last ten years' work which affords protection to those whose earnings may drop in the final year. There are some jobs in Britain, such as manual labourers and dentists, where the earnings profile peaks at forty and in those cases some uprated average salary scheme must be introduced. One extra point should be made; salary means PAYE earnings and not basic pay; many people have retired not on 50 per cent earnings as expected but 30 per cent because their take-home pay was made up of high non-pensionable elements including overtime, shift rates or commission. However care must be taken to see that employees whose non-basic salary elements drop, near to retirement date, do not overpay for their pension. This occurs when contributions are based on the higher rate but the pension on the lower one in a final salary-type pension scheme.

A new trend in pensions is emerging as the basic company strategy – the integrated pension. The rationale of this is that people will have only one pension amounting at maximum to two-thirds of pensionable salary, not the two pensions, one state and one occupational.

The Inland Revenue rules permit an occupational pension of two-thirds of salary at time of retirement as well as a state pension. Thus in an integrated scheme as the state pension rises, the total pension remains constant, i.e., the company pension element decreases. As the state pension represents a high percentage of salary for the lower paid this measure mitigates strongly against low-paid employees. It is however now prevalent and will require firm action by the trade union movement to prevent it spreading further, before even attempting the task of reversal. The new legislation however may inspire more rather than fewer integrated schemes 'riding on top' of a 'contracted in' pension.

The second ploy being tried by managements is the voluntary pension scheme, generally across the total body of employees of the enterprise. This has two effects. The first is to refuse negotiations on the ground that the scheme is not a condition of service. The second is to pitch the scheme at a lower level and thus save money. This is achieved because manual workers generally outnumber staff and because manual workers traditionally have not been as interested or militant on pension matters as white-collar unions. This ploy has been used by GEC and Dowty Rotol and seems favoured by General Motors, and there is a general move to 'single status' often using the pension scheme as the main lever.

The basics

Having attempted to clear management-inspired hurdles the scheme remains to be negotiated – so back to the basics. Pensions should accrue at the rate of 1/60 of pensionable salary per year of service giving an occupational pension of two-thirds salary after forty years' service and having these right makes all the difference to the fringe benefits. A dependant's pension of two-thirds of the prime pension plus junior dependants' allowances should be paid as of right in the event of death in retirement. A lump sum of a minimum of twice salary plus a dependant's pension should be paid in the event of death in service.

A good scheme should also include long-term disability and ill-health provisions; a commutation of the pension into a lump sum of one-and-a-half times final salary; early retirement at age sixty without actuarial reduction and no discrimination against women. Women have lost out in pension terms through a combination of Government legislation, actuarial calculations and lack of pressure. Many schemes have not been open to women; many more are in schemes which give them inferior benefits. Some schemes actively discriminate inasmuch as men's pensions accrue at 1/60 per year, with women's at 1/80 per year. In nearly all schemes there is a differential in retirement age of sixty-five for men and sixty for women. The result is that women have five years less to accrue rights and thus get a lower pension, but they must live on a low sum for five years more than a man. In addition women, on average, live longer than men so that women in retirement are often condemned to poverty. The Sex Discrimination Act and the new pensions legislation now make it obligatory for occupational schemes to treat men and women equally as far as access, basic benefits and date of joining are concerned.

The reasons for the difference in retirement age are historically based on relative marriage ages and are now no longer relevant either statistically or socially. There is no reason why there should not be a common retirement age of sixty in all occupational schemes as no legislative changes are necessary although it is expensive. Schemes were not allowed to provide for widowers' pensions for their women members by the Inland Revenue unless extraordinary circumstances obtained. This quite indefensible position was recently changed but in turn the number of schemes which provide this benefit as of right can be counted on the fingers of one hand. The argument against equality in a scheme is that it invokes an element of cross-subsidy from men to women. There are however many examples of this which have no reference to women and no-one complains; single men subsidise married men, married men subsidise others with large families and, in a simplistic sense, in the real world a rate-paying, non-reader subsidises a heavy library user. Yet no one complains.

The pension scheme is not yet complete. Dynamism or inflation-proofing of pensions in payment must be written in. This can take several forms. In the public sector, e.g. the civil service or the NHS, the Exchequer makes up any fund deficiency and thus pensions can be linked to the retail price index. A scheme without such a provision is open-ended and would require the employer to top-up. A good situation links the pension to the salary of the man currently doing the job of the retired man or its nearest equivalent although this may be dangerous if the job ceases to exist. Another good method is to negotiate pensioners' increases at the same time as the wage round thus giving the employer and the employee, as future pensioner, some measure of control. The drawback in this case is that most procedure agreements do not contain a clause allowing for negotiations on a group of workers called pensioners. However the Employee Protection legislation should overcome this old problem. Two final, less satisfactory, but more common methods are trustees' discretionary awards and a fixed percentage increase, generally set at 3 per cent per annum.

This whole matter is admittedly costly to a company but one consolation is that if there is continued general inflation which necessitates such action, equity and gilt prices have inflated proportionately and returns to the scheme are correspondingly higher than anticipated. The scheme can generally afford it over the long-term. The new legislation which will take all pensions up to the minimum standard inflation-proofed in 1978 will be of great help in negotiating full inflation proofing if only because it will be easier administratively. In addition to this the Government is prepared to aid schemes which comply with the new regulations.

Boards of management

A non-cost item is the question of who runs the scheme. Occupational pensions can be either self-funded, or self-run but with investment made by a bank, or sold to the employer as a package arrangement by insurance companies, unit trusts or merchant banks. In any event the monies are held in trust for members of the scheme. The trust deed constrains the trustees in some ways, but also gives them immense powers over investment policies if applicable and distribution of benefits. On occasion a bank acts as trustee, but more normally the trustees are appointed by the company in a most paternalistic way. The money in the fund is the employees' own money (held in trust) and as such there should be no argument that, at the least, trustees must be divided into one-half management appointees and one-half trades union elected. The Government has reinforced this attitude by recommending 50 per cent member participation on boards of management in a 1976 White Paper. Fortunately most major companies have already seen this point: both Ford's and Chrysler's conceded this principle in negotiations. The public sector has had it in operation for twenty-five years.

Trade unions will have to train these management board representatives. There are statutory duties laid upon trustees, for example, most trust deeds have a clause which states that the trustees must act in a way which benefits those members of the scheme for whom the monies are held in trust. This obviously circumscribes trustee actions although it is possible to argue that this rule has not been obeyed by a board of trustees in the past.

Obviously the duties of trustees and their discretionary duties relating to the disbursement of benefits will have to be taught. The major bone of contention will however be the investment policy of the scheme. There have recently been revelations about pension fund investment managers moving into the art world and the North America property market. It could be argued, and many unions will argue, that such investments are not only socially unacceptable but also act against the interests of scheme members.

There is a general agreement in Britain that manufacturing industry needs a greater share of available investment than it has received over the past decade. If monies are not channelled into this sector but continue to be allocated to the stranger areas of investment and to both government securities and the short-term money markets there will ultimately be fewer and fewer jobs available in any sector. There is thus a difference in approach which can be based on a time-scale, the long-term viability of the British economy or a short-term, high-return approach.

Unions such as ASTMS intend to provide an investment advisory service to its members' trustees. It will be professionally produced and will also be socially based, bearing in mind the primary duty to provide good pensions.

Portable pensions

The final point to establish in a good scheme is transferability or preservation. Very few employees start with one employer with whom they work their whole lifetime; most leave, willingly or unwillingly and change jobs several times. The types of schemes that have been mentioned assume that an employee will continue working through to retirement and get a maximum pension. This is rare. When a person leaves service with a company he or she needs three options. The worst is to withdraw his own contributions (with interest). This method loses all the employer's contributions (these have to stay in the fund) and after 1975 this method will only be allowable for those who have less than five years continuous service. The second option should be a preserved pension, payable at retirement date; and the final option a transferred pension to the new employer. Although a transferred pension or transferability seem the most attractive and best method, in practice there is little to choose between it and preservation. What unfortunately happens is that the transfer value enters the new scheme, but is just put on one side, that is to say, it is merely preserved in a different scheme. True transferability is rare outside of the public sector or special bilateral pacts between large, private companies and public corporations.

The result of this is that pensioners often find themselves with a far lower pension than they expected. If a preserved pension is not inflation-proofed the employee loses money. It is that simple. Employers dislike transferability. Talks were held with the Engineering Employers Federation in the early 1970s on the practicality of some form of transfer system but these broke down when it became apparent that the Federation had not the slightest interest in constructing such a scheme. Not only would the employers have lost their tying element with employees, but it would also have cost them additional monies. Most schemes depend on people moving out of the scheme because if the money stays behind interest can be earned and thus less money need be provided by the employer. There have been very many forfeits of the employer's contributions into schemes on the part of the contributor who leaves taking only his own contributions with him. A further difficulty is that some types of schemes are incompatible with others and transfer values have to be worked out. An example is transferring from a money-purchase type of scheme, to a final-salary type scheme. The transfer value is often smaller than anticipated; this arose in 1973 with the new British Airways pension scheme and transfers in from the smaller airlines. There is a major transfer club in the public sector amongst the NHS, civil service, teaching, Medical Research Council, etc., but to date this has not been fully extended to the private sector, nor exploited by it.

If you manage to have all the above points in a pension scheme it should provide a reasonable standard of living when retired. Meanwhile, occupational pensions are very big business and some of the consequences of that size can be unpleasant. An insurance company has to guarantee benefits and thus to protect its investments may seek to influence managements on their employment policies.

Big business can also affect the self-funded scheme. There are no laws in Britain regulating self-investment through pension funds, it is a favoured way of thwarting take-over bids as it gives company control over a hidden block of shares. Worse still there is no law stopping a pension fund buying the company properties and revaluing, leasing back at low rents or whatever suits the company's financial policy. If the company goes into liquidation, pension liabilities may not be met although the new legislation will ameliorate this problem and conceivably prevent it happening. Not only is an employee dependent on the company in his working life, but after retirement too. Amendments drafted to stop these practices were defeated in the Committee stages of the Social Security Bill.

Unions must protect and fight for pensioners. They must do it through classic negotiating machinery. To do otherwise would be an abdication of responsibility to members at a time when it should be exercised the most. In addition the trade unions must take full advantage of the potential offered by 50 per cent of the boards of management of pension schemes. This should not be seen as conflicting with the collective bargaining arrangements, as the two functions can be separated. Retirement must not mean genteel poverty at best; it should be a sensible reward for a lifetime of service and often a lifetime of making profits for others.

Chapter 9

The environment

'*Dark satanic mills*' – Blake

Depletion and pollution

There is only one earth. In and on earth are raw materials in finite amounts. These include air, water, soil, ore-bearing rocks and fossil fuel deposits; each of these have a finite quantum. Therein lies the crux of the environmental problem. If air, water and soil could be regenerated, pollution would be a transitory irritant only and resource depletion would become a science fiction.

It is a fact that the environmental problem hits hardest on the lower paid. The cheap areas for urban living tend to be the drabbest, dirtiest and most polluted, for the richer can afford to move into a better environment. If costs of goods and services rise because of resource depletion, the richer will afford the goods or services, the poorer will have to do without.

The lower paid work in bad environmental conditions and the rich in pleasant surroundings. If Britain is smoggy the rich can fly to a non-smoggy part of the world – the poorer, that is the employed, have no such options.

Trade unions have always been involved in negotiations and lobbying about the environment inside and outside the factories and offices. The Lancashire and Yorkshire textile unions gained their original cohesion not just through agitation on wages but through the alarm created by 'steaming' and other unsavoury work-practices within the mills. The NUM has fought, and is still fighting, a basic battle against pneumoconiosis and other health hazards in the pits. The in-work environment has properly been a preserve of the trade union movement in the past and continues to be so. Strangely, as old techniques die and new industrial forms and products take their place the hazards increase, not least because of the unknown properties of the materials concerned.

New insecticides and new nuclear developments all contain the seeds of personal and generalised disaster. A major company's insecticide division does toxicity testing of new products and from time to time departments have had urgent messages to destroy all traces of the substance. However, in the meantime personnel might have been exposed to a danger. Carcinomas and other malignant growths tend to be on the increase but the result of exposure to a carcinogen may not manifest itself for many years, thus the proving of cause and effect to the satisfaction of the courts and the DHSS is a long, drawn-out affair. Many people may well die unnecessarily, and indeed, as a result of provable neglect, in the interim.

Deafness, ulcers, cardiac problems, arthritis and mutilations can be traced in some degree to the in-work environment. Trade unions *do* negotiate on these topics but with marginal success and, unfortunately, we still work in a compensation rather than prevention system. Money is paid on a listed basis for loss of toes, feet, legs, arms, inability to breathe properly, see properly, or hear adequately. The proper objective must be to prevent these accidents happening in the first place.

In-work environment

Working conditions are not just a fit and proper subject for a continental-style works committee to discuss and cogitate about. This is a subject for overall pressures, industrial and otherwise. Knowledge is the first essential as many employers are still not sensitive to the dangers and there is an inadequate overall, personal alertness. Companies do not take favourably to public coverage of the fact they are crippling or killing employees although their sensitivity stems from the paternal influence which still pervades so much of British management. If the public were made aware of the damage created a groundswell of opinion would both force the company to change its policy and also inform and create a militant feeling for protection in an organised way.

Industrial action on the in-work environment is not unknown in Britain or in the United States. A pit in South Wales (opened in 1960) had strikes every week about dangerous water-levels until it finally had to close in 1968. Shell workers in the United States have had strikes over the handling of chemicals and strikes over the handling of materials. The strikes at the Chrysler and Fiat plants in the USA and Italy were basically over the in-work environment although in these cases automated techniques led to complete job boredom and alienation and in the USA, to vehicle damage by a disenchanted young workforce in a 'greenfield' automobile assembly plant.

115

Unions on the general environment

The environment is not confined to in-work and nor should a trade union's concern be limited to this area alone. The TGWU have recently developed a new and important technique. They have extrapolated from the in-work environment in two separate cases. The Rio Tinto plant at Avonmouth was found to have dangerously high lead levels within the plant, resulting in lead poisoning in several employees. Having determined the cause which seemed derived from a cost-cutting exercise, the TGWU then traced the effects caused by the discharge of effluent containing these high lead levels on the local ecology. The result was that the union was then supported by local environmentalist groups; the pressure on RTZ became that much more powerful and diffused and the union won. Workers in a plant in Lambeth were found to have excessively high lead levels in their blood. The TGWU then persuaded the local Medical Officer of Health to test the lead levels in local children; these also proved to be high due to atmospheric pollution from the plant chimneys. The resultant publicity closed the factory until the necessary screening devices had been installed. Without the external work it sparked off it is doubtful if the union would have succeeded.

These cautionary tales throw up the first of the problems. Can a trade union in defence of its workers close a plant and thereby lose them their livelihood? The trade-off is physical well-being as against material *and* physical well-being. The answer must surely be that the plant must close, but that the union must take all the available steps to ensure that it re-opens or alternative employment is provided. A union which ignores the physical dangers to its members in order to keep them in work is an accomplice in potential grievous bodily harm although the perpetrator of the crime is the employer. Lobbying of Government agencies may have to take a place in this process and here a well-organised Parliamentary presence is also essential.

The importance of the TGWU gambits must not be overlooked. Let us reverse the process and consider the industrial effluent, both air and water-borne in South Wales, Billingham, the Potteries, Motherwell and other highly-developed, industrial complexes. If the environment is murky on the outside, what is it like for the workers on the inside? If hazards exist on the outside what is the physical state of those who have to spend not only their leisure hours in close approximation to the source of the pollution but have to spend their residual hours inside the source? A fruitful area for investigation exists but such investigations require time, specialised skills and money. Neither the DHSS nor the Department of Environment show any inclination to provide such monies. Indeed the new National Health Re-organisation Act specifically shunts industrial medicine into the province of the Department of Employment and from there to the Manpower Services Commission and they believe that the Health and Safety Executive Inspectorate and the Employment Medical Advisory Service cover this field. Local Authorities have some statutory duties but little interest in, or money to promote research. The Department appears to be the only body in Britain (outside of employers) who are happy with this arrangement. If independent bodies do not come forward, the trade union movement must start to undertake this research, using the TUC as a co-ordinating body.

Legislation

There is however a glimmer of hope on all these fronts. The Health and Safety at Work Act was placed on the statute book in 1974 and this gives employees a framework within which they can influence the in-work environment. It is by no means a perfect piece of legislation because it is woolly and infested with the delaying words 'so far as is reasonably practicable' which have a history of emasculating good Parliamentary intentions. However this major defect not-withstanding the Act makes a major conceptual leap forward in that it enshrines the proposition that employees have a right to know about and to do something about their environmental working conditions.

Basically, the Act is an enabling law which sets up the Health and Safety Commission, the Health and Safety Executive, safety representatives, provides for 'codes of practice', and the Employment Advisory Medical Service. Employers have to provide written statements of their health and safety policy to employees, have a duty to safeguard the health and safety of employees including research into the handling and carriage of substances where this has been unknown before and to tell the employees about these substances. The Health and Safety Commission and Executive (which have trade union representatives on them) have the task of making arrangements for research, training and information, drafting regulations and orders, advising the Secretary of State and directing investigations and enquiries. The legislation will be fleshed out with health and safety Regulations and Codes of Practice and it is on these that the test of how effective this particular legislation and the Commission will reside. This side of the Act enables trade unions to influence Regulations and Codes by making approaches to the

Commission either of an initiatory nature or through a more technical and detailed submission.

However the delays in laying Regulations before Parliament are creating a malaise that can only be offset by determined local union action.

This is one arm of the legislation which will affect trade unions. The other is the appointment of safety representatives or stewards to represent health and safety matters to management at individual plants and the setting up of joint management–worker safety committees. It will be the duty of an employer to consult safety representatives on the making of, or the maintenance of, health and safety programmes. Given the newly-emerging representatives, arrangements on the lines of basic bargaining procedure agreements should not be far behind and under this umbrella there must be detailed negotiations on the in-work environment. This will be the second arm of unions' involvement.

Within the Act the provisions for an increased number of factory inspectors, and the centralising of all the different inspectorates under the Commission (with the exception of Local Authority Inspectorates) has obviously to be welcomed. However, money must be found to improve the service as suggested and there is no sign that this is forthcoming in sufficient quantity; the same, unfortunately, applies to the Employment Medical Advisory Service. But the Act opens up new avenues for trade unions and their members to explore, provided that a serious and concerted effort is made to make the most of the opportunity offered and, as with pensions, on a joint-union basis.

Diminishing resources and jobs

Pollution is one arm of the environmental gorgon; the other is resource depletion. Both create grave problems for the trade union movement. It is too easy to seek to restrict the motor car, ban Concorde, close oil refineries, and try to build an airport elsewhere. The car, Concorde, oil refineries, airports, all provide individuals with employment and all add to the money circulating in the economy on which the multiplier works, creating more jobs, etc. Replacing the motor car by electric cars and a more comprehensive, cheaper transport system would cut down on both pollution and slow resource depletion. It could also put people out of work. Do trade unions bow to the short-term or take a long-term initiative?

Before any discussion of the environment can take place it is necessary to take a brief look at the arguments involved in resource depletion. The 'doommongers' proclaim that the world's resources

118

are being used up at an alarming rate. They point to the growth of population, the fossil fuel shortage and, above all, the push to industrial growth. The Club of Rome/MIT report, based on available and projected statistics, openly argued that the only hope for mankind was zero growth. The input may have been faulty, technology may have been discounted, but the logic has not been seriously challenged. The optimists say and argue that technology has always solved our problems or 'necessity is the mother of invention'. Furthermore, if a material depletes and thus rises in cost, it will become less commercially viable and society will accept a substitute, e.g., soya-bean steaks instead of real meat.

It is certain that no trade union could countenance zero growth in the economy; indeed, a society which achieved that position would be so primitive and probably based on the commune system, and would not need trade unions. On the other hand can a union take the chance that, in producing more cars, providing more jobs, it is only hastening the end of the employment of its members because of increased oil consumption?

Social responsibilities and negotiations

Unions have a duty to their members not only to react to the short-term situation. Both pollution and resource problems invoke the concept of social cost and social profit; in a sense we need a three-dimensional accounting system and this is a matter for Governments and trade unions to take a firm position on environmental issues. For almost the first time, the movement will have to take a positive and long-term strategic position.

The new social remuneration packages that trade unions negotiate go beyond simply wages and hours. These bargains go into areas affecting not only the employee, but the employee's family, for example, low-cost mortgages and holiday travel. This concept must be extended to the environment. Trade union action will have to be applied along at least two, distinct fronts starting with the interfaces of employer and governmental agencies.

The first premise is that the polluter must pay. There is nearly always some cost in pollution control although it must be stressed, not always. For example, a study of paper mills in the USA showed that those whose pollution (mainly water) was least made the highest profits, or where there is drinkable water there is a return. The newer mills, with more modern equipment obviously had a higher return on capital. There is thus often an advantage to the pollution producer to cut down pollution. The cost of pollution control, whether it is for a control device, alternate material use or an

119

alternate technology, must be borne by the polluter. However, this while defensible in principle, is very difficult to enforce in practice.

If a producer of goods or services is confronted by an increase in costs, the price of the commodity invariably rises. Thus the polluter does not pay a penny, the public who purchase foot the bill and unless it is a genuine luxury item the cost is bound to be regressive, i.e., bear more heavily on the lower paid. Alternatively, the government could subsidise the producer either directly or through the taxation and investment-grant system. Unless the base of British taxation changes, this cost, too, will be borne by the lower paid and even more so since the introduction of VAT. There might be novel ways whereby ordinary men and women would not bear most of the costs.

Consider this idea: if all the TUC-affiliated unions arranged to take concerted action each plant responsible for creating the pollution could have the cost of pollution control worked out by a central body. The cost could then be broken down into a cost per head of employee. The unions would then claim double that amount before the pollution is controlled. If the controls are operative before a due date, say twelve months after the claim, the claim is reduced to half of its original amount. It is a stick and carrot method. The stick is the penalty of increased costs which will *not* reduce real income. The carrot is that an enterprise which controls pollution will then have a cost advantage over those in the same industry who do not. It will pay to be clean. This is not, incidentally, an argument for generalised central bargaining. It is merely a method of determining compensation whilst using collective bargaining to create a situation where compensation is not necessary. It is not applicable in any other field.

Government and supranational action

The second avenue is the pressure on the Government to sponsor alternate technology research so that closures of environmentally damaging plants would be swiftly followed by newer, more socially-oriented production. One cannot deny that the internal combustion engine has a lot to answer for, yet where is the electric car, where is the gas car? If central heating is using up an incredible amount of resources why not try solar energy?

If trade unions balk at this prospect they will be condemning their members and their families (including the unborn members) to a life of environmental deprivation. Do we really want to be in a position where a pay increase is spent on oxygen to breathe, as in Tokyo? Do we really want to perpetuate a system where money wages may increase, real material living standards may increase, yet at both work and at leisure there are more hazards and more pressures?

Britain is not isolated from the rest of the world. Not only do we suffer forms of pollution from other countries, both air-borne and sea-borne, but we compete with them too. Whether expenditure is on the in-work or general environment it adds to the cost of production and thus the more enlightened countries with good social legislation suffer a comparative disadvantage. This is a matter for international trade union action – action which has now been initiated.

Bargaining is not only about money. Bargaining is also about being kept alive and healthy to enjoy the fruits of going to work in an industrialised society and this is the challenge to us all.

Chapter 10

Multi-nationals and the European Economic Community

'*Workers of the world unite*' – Marx

Introduction

British entry into the European Economic Community created new problems for trade unions and multiplied many old ones. Britain has always been a world-trading nation; importing and exporting have been a way of life for centuries but are now even more critical to our economic survival. We import approximately 50 per cent of our total foodstuffs and vast quantities of raw materials, such as iron ore, oil, wood and metal-bearing ores. In order to pay for these, Britain has to export manufactured goods (in the era before our own offshore hydro-carbon exploitation). This has given us wide contact with the outside world, despite the potential insularity geography imposed on Britain before the air routes were established. Because of trading ties abroad British industry and commerce expanded and invested overseas, initially in the old Empire and South America, but latterly almost anywhere; however, the earnings on capital rarely returned to Britain and represented a net outflow. In the times of Commonwealth preference and cheap, raw materials Britain could survive, but now we have entered the EEC with a net outflow of capital the balance of trade and payments seem destined for a long, negative spell.

British entry into the EEC thus confronts trade unions with two basically different problems. The long-term effects of an economic nature on its members, not only working in Britain but also in the EEC, and the political institutions to which the trade unions will ultimately have to adjust (if Britain remains a member) and the alien type of bureaucracy which has emerged.

The multi-national company poses different problems; the similarity between the EEC and a multi-national starts and ends just six miles off the British coast. Their lack of accountability, their desire to transfer capital resources (including employees) around the world, their sheer economic weight and consequent political leverage make them a potential danger to Governments and trade unions alike. To ignore either the EEC or multi-national companies is an abdication of a trade union's responsibilities to its members. This does not imply any approval of either the EEC or multi-national companies, nor does it argue for formal ties with EEC machinery; indeed, as we shall see, it is almost impossible for a single British trade union to have meaningful contacts with any aspect of the Community.

The EEC and the large market

The European Economic Community (a misnomer on two counts, it does not pretend to represent all Europe and it is as social and political as economic) consists of nine European countries in a formal and rigid association sanctified by a treaty of accession. The eventual aim is to have full economic and political union of the nine, but this must perforce entail the 'harmonisation' of not only fiscal and monetary matters but also social mores, consumer tastes, social security and political institutions; in short the whole of society. If this sounds radical or alarmist let us examine the trends.

If the wish is to administer a large market fairly, the first pre-requisite is that the manufacturers should have roughly the same advantages and disadvantages as each other. In the past such comparative advantages have been dealt with by general agreement on trade and tariffs regulations and individual national tariffs, but the EEC abolishes tariffs between members, although it seeks to live behind tariff walls to keep out the advantaged invader such as Japan. To guarantee that employers work within the same constraints one must have food at the same price, full mobility of labour and full monetary union to prevent one currency getting an advantage, while social security and health-service payments and benefits have to be harmonised because they represent a part of real income. On the question of tastes and mores a market the size of the EEC works on the principle of the economies of scale given by its size or seeks to emulate an American concept. If this market were split into smaller, autonomous markets, these economies would not be achieved. For example, the French grow mainly soft wheat which makes the typical crusty loaf, while French women are not in the labour force to the extent of British women, so that a twice-daily visit to the baker's is feasible. It is likely that this loaf will become the community standard, and that both tastes and customs will

123

have to change in Britain. The same applies to beer. The British pint of bitter is live and brewed in a different way to the Continental light beers; it has already been decided to adopt the Continental method as the Community beer after a ten-year interval. These are the small side-effects our membership may well induce, but as they affect the standard and quality of living of the British employee that is very much a trade union concern. The output arrangements in industries such as steel or electronic computers pose different threats. They are, however, long-term problems. The immediate effect is that decisions are being taken in Brussels which affect all the British, employers and employees alike, and which are taken in a vacuum as far as the British are concerned.

EEC government

The first point to note in the EEC is that it is a totally different method of government to that which has evolved in Britain. Here the Government is the executive arm and is drawn from the majority party; the civil service provides the briefs whilst policies have previously been put to the electorate by the ruling party. The chain of responsibility is that a minister is responsible to the Houses of Parliament and the members responsible to the electorate; there is no doctrine of civil service responsibility, they are technocrats (in theory) serving their political masters. The EEC arrangement is totally different; the Commission, which is the equivalent of our civil service, instigates policy and is charged with carrying this policy through to completion, yet is responsible to no directly-elected body. The decision-making body is the Council of Ministers, with one minister per member country and the Commission policies are either ratified or amended at this Council. The European Parliament which is on the sidelines, currently has no legislative or executive power. Even the possibility of direct elections to this Parliament appears to offer the appearance rather than the practice of accountability. The EEC system is more like the French system, of weak government plus a highly qualified civil service, than the British system of strong government. The unions tend to get absorbed into this system and be diminished by it.

The focus of all EEC-watchers in Brussels is the Commission itself. It is divided into thirteen different Commissariats with each one having at least two directors – general and directorates, sundry directors, deputy directors and 'functionaires', amounting to almost 5,500 staff members. The Commission has certain committees, the largest of which is the Economic and Social Committee which has advisory powers only; in addition, there is the Standing Committee on Employment and one on Agriculture: these are known as the tri-partite committees.

Union representational difficulties

The Commission has taken the decision to recognise certain trade union alliances for consultative purposes very much as the Americans allow registered bodies and lobbyists. To be recognised one must have a European structure and not just a national base. The recognised union organisations are the European Confederation of Trade Unions to which the British TUC is affiliated and the European-based trade secretariats spun off by the traditional international secretariats for (say) metal or transport workers. Unless an individual union becomes multi-national, it cannot be recognised and will not be consulted by the Commission before decisions are taken. The theory is that each union will be affiliated to a body which has recognition. Thus, the chain of lobbying would be for a British union to approach the TUC on a specific issue of interest to its members, e.g., harmonisation of medical qualifications. If the TUC consider it of interest they will have to influence the ETUC. If the ETUC consider it important enough they will represent that view to the relevant directorate in the Commission.

There is a chance, of course, that the subject may be presented to the Economic and Social Committee or one of its sub-committees. The TUC nominate directly to the EEC and although it has only an advisory capacity the union views could be made known through this channel. The problem is that substitutes or extra delegation members are not permitted, and some topics are, by their nature, extremely complex and technical. It has been tentatively suggested that the TUC could circulate the lists of topics which are on the agenda for discussion. But the weight of paper-handling this would entail rules it out very early on.

The TUC has eight seats out of a total of 144 on this committee alone. The committee is then divided into nine sections, each of which have from 30 to 60 members, covering the whole range of a national or supranational body's activities. The demands made on a busy General Council member (and General Secretary) are enormous and when overnight stays in Brussels are taken into account, it may well mean five days per month or a quarter of available working time. Whether this can be justified is doubtful and in the longer run the TUC may not feel that the return they are getting for this involvement is justified and reduce this commitment, thus diminishing the committee's role.

One example of the problems that the Brussels-committees

system can pose is that of energy. There is an Energy and Nuclear Affairs Sub-Committee of the Economic and Social Committee; the Energy Sub-Committee of the European Trades Union Confederation; the Energy Committee of the European Coal and Steel Committee on Coal-Mining. Each of these acts individually, but often with the same delegates, discussing the same subjects at slightly different times and under different secretariats.

The British system is more direct as, if a problem on medical qualifications arose, the union would approach the DHSS both directly and through its Parliamentary Committee. If legislation was pending it would attempt to amend the Bill at its Committee stage. In the EEC direct action of this type is impossible. The course of action for the EEC might be to approach the Secretary of State for Health and Social Security who could ask the Foreign Secretary to veto or alter the proposal at the Council of Ministers' stage. Although theoretically possible, even the most fanatical supporter of the EEC constitution would deem it unlikely.

In Britain, trade unions are accustomed to having not only positive lobbying facilities, but also to sponsoring MPs. This does not make the Member a captive of the union (far from it), but it does argue a certain identity of philosophy and outlook which can profitably be used by both sides to further their shared political and economic ends. On the other side of the House, industry and finance is well represented by company chairmen and directors and these operate in roughly the same way. Our entry to the EEC has virtually stopped the effectiveness of these traditional manoeuvres; only on those matters reserved to Britain (and these will be progressively fewer and fewer) will lobbying be directly effective.

Information

If one cannot lobby there is still information needed in order to operate. A trade union must know what is happening in the EEC, must know European legislation, must be aware of the Commission drafts, must have the political line-up on each proposal and thus be able to assess its chances of passing the Council of Ministers substantially unaltered. It must be acquainted with these papers in order to be able to take the appropriate action on behalf of its members and to try to pre-empt rather than react. Information is available in Britain from four sources. ASTMS has a private consultancy with a telex link which can give quick, accurate and personalised information. The EEC information office in London has a selection of official EEC documents, but unfortunately these are often late and sometimes in French and on occasion, documents which have been reported in the Press are not available at any time. On the subject of information on 26 September 1973 the House of Lords made a plea for more information going as far as suggesting a 'spy in Brussels'. In evidence before a Lords Committee, Mr John Davies the then Chancellor of the Duchy of Lancaster with special responsibilities for Europe said that there was a problem with 'documents where there is apparently not a right of access and where, in fact, if they were revealed without the proper confidence of the Commission being respected that is a specific breach of confidentiality.' One should notice that this is a civil service withholding documents from the executive and legislature; trade unions are not alone in having information problems.

The social affairs Directorate is one on which some trade unions can represent themselves. The Directorate sponsors the bi-partite committees of the industrial relations section. These committees are formed under the aegis of the Commission and are designed to allow for meetings of the unions of the nine with the employers of the nine in a specific industry. The committees, to date, have concentrated in the traditional industry areas, agriculture, coal mining, railways, trawling, etc., and they are often single-union situations. The eventual aim of these committees is to negotiate a European-wide procedure agreement and uniform conditions of service. The newer industries of electronics, air transport or complex metal-working are multi-employer, multi-union situations and at present it is not possible to envisage how the system will cope with them. In addition, Britain is the only one of the nine with a well-developed and genuine white-collar private sector union system and this will have to be taken into account should the bi-partite committees tackle the modern industrial world.

Mobility of labour and union problems

Meanwhile, in specific terms, what will membership of the EEC mean for trade union work and collective bargaining outside of the change in general economic conditions consequent upon the Common Agricultural Policy, the Regional Policy and full monetary integration? Two specific proposals affect British trade unions; the first is the free mobility of labour and the second, the directive on worker participation.

Free mobility of labour presupposes harmonised standards of education, training and qualifications, for without these there can be no real interchange. Mobility brings with it new issues. If British workers go to work in France on, say, the Concorde, who will represent them, their British union or a French union?

In a cross-frontier, mobility situation, can a union represent pockets of its members in Essen, Naples and Copenhagen? The answer would seem to be links and reciprocal arrangements with other EEC unions or even amalgamations of differing national unions. Both are possible. ASTMS has many such agreements which cover the world and, indeed, represent members without such arrangements working mainly in telecommunications and airlines in, amongst others, California, Hong Kong, Bermuda, the Seychelles – in fact in all five continents, although almost all the contracts are settled in the United Kingdom. Nevertheless, if mobility is to take place on a larger scale than hitherto either multi-lingual, multi-national, peripatetic union officials will emerge or reciprocal agreements will be forgone.

Whilst on the subject of mobility, it is just as well to note the phenomenon of migrant workers. Germany has a chronic labour shortage and 'imported' workers from Spain, Portugal, Turkey, Algeria and Yugoslavia amongst others. These workers have neither the rights of migrant EEC nationals, nor do they receive benefits similar to them. They have, in some countries, represented a 'threat' to trade unions and living standards in the same way that low-paid women and non-patrial Commonwealth workers do in Britain. In addition, their conditions have been degradingly low. If this occurs in Britain, the trade union movement must not shun these workers; it must recruit them and negotiate for them. In some countries they are (notably in West Germany) being induced to go back to their countries of origin as a response to economic depression and rising unemployment.

The common multi-national

The second fork of the international scene confronting a trade union intent on bargaining for its members in the most effective way is the multi-national company. Although multi-nationals have been in existence for many years, it is only in the past decade of accelerating technology that their role in given states has been analysed and their stunning impact on world economy fully realised. Marx wrote, 'Workers of the world unite, you have nothing to lose but your chains' and the multi-nationals have adapted this to, 'Employers of the world unite, you cannot lose, you must gain.' Why is it that the multi-national company has become such a threat to trade unions? Because they are so all-pervasive in their market dominance in the key sectors, from food to vehicles to data-retrieval.

Effects on unions

Multi-national companies affect collective bargaining in two main ways – both indirectly and directly. The indirect effect is simply that of currency manipulations and its effects on the Pound sterling, and thus inflation. A multi-national company is able to transfer vast amounts of money around the world; at any one time a major US multi-national company may be holding thousands of millions of dollars in liquid form. Bills have to be met at specified intervals, but there are often lead and lag times between the receipt of the money and the due date for payment. A company that does not invest this in the currency that gives it the best return compatible with low risk makes a real loss. When the Pound is floating the balance-of-payment figures have an important psychological effect on the currency speculators who handle these multi-national funds. If sterling falls, the multi-nationals pull out and switch to the Mark, Swiss Franc or Yen. This has the effect of devaluing the Pound even further and thus contributing to inflation in Britain. In an effort to restore stability, interest rates rise in the hope that a greater return will compensate for the risk, but although this may stabilise the currency it results in dearer mortgages, overdrafts and business finance (investment). If this sounds familiar think of the months April to October in 1973, June 1975 and the summer and autumn of 1976. Inflation without commensurate salary increases led to a loss of real income and a cut in employees' standards of living and this affects collective bargaining in as much as union demands are justifiably that much greater.

The direct effects are information gaps and potential or actual asset transfers. As outlined, a trade union prepares a claim based on several factors, cost of living, comparability, profitability, etc., but when negotiating with a multi-national company and often when bargaining with a conglomerate, it is almost impossible to determine the precise profitability of the company without a full-scale investigation. There are several reasons for this lack of essential information.

Multi-national gambits

Multi-national companies are regular users of tax havens for the registration of their companies (one of them has a head office in Curaçao). This means that total net profit on a world basis is almost impossible to discover. Does one look at the profits of Ford UK, for example, or Ford Europe or Ford world wide, based in Detroit, when negotiating a salary claim in Britain? The arguments for basing a claim on world profits are compelling. Let us use an un-named American-owned motor manufacturer with subsidiaries in Britain, Europe and Asia as an example.

Cars and commercial vehicles are produced in Britain. Accounts are drawn up and deposited at Companies House each year, but the company is not public in Britain and no annual report or responsibility to shareholders is involved. The accounts show a small profit with a tiny percentage return on capital employed and in the annual wage round the management plead poverty and state that the claimed increase would convert this profit and a healthy return on capital. Is the British subsidiary really being run as a social service to British employees as the management suggest? Almost certainly not. The following gambits have been used in the past by, amongst others, multi-national motor manufacturers; all are real, none theoretical.

A multi-national producer can use its plants to manufacture components which are not used in the assembly of the final product in that country, but are shipped to a company plant in another country and assembled there. Although this sounds expensive in freight charges, if the company owns the means of transport, it can be made virtually cost free and in any event such costs are a small percentage of total costs. The profit is made in the following ways, all depending on differing corporate tax systems and differing dates of tax demands. For example, the company assembles cars in Britain but the chassis of some of them are manufactured in Germany or another European country. At what price are these chassis bought? It could be a very high one giving a large profit in Germany (a comparatively low-tax area) and a loss in Britain (which was a high-tax area). The total profit to the company is higher than it would have been if the cars had been manufactured and assembled in their respective countries. Why did a major US-owned company cancel the contracts of thirty-eight different British component manufacturers and substitute for them with foreign-owned suppliers with thirty-one of the components rising in price as a consequence? Who owned these foreign component firms?

At least two car manufacturers produce engines in Britain destined for the companies' 'compact' cars in the American market. At what price are these engines sold? There is no way of finding out from published accounts and one suspects the figure is considerably under commercial levels; in other words a transfer price has been internally settled. It can actually pay a company in global terms to maintain a British subsidiary which, if not running at a loss, then does not *have* to make a profit. One cannot even take the sales of cars or sewing machines or cans of food as an index of performance because of the high percentage of products transferred to overseas plants; because of this and the transfer price system, revenue is not a reliable indicator of surplus.

The Employment Protection Act which provides for the disclosure of information necessary for collective bargaining purposes may not be sufficient to embrace these problems. If the parent company is registered overseas, unions would need an order making its internal accounting procedures available. Although the Code of Practice has not yet been published it is doubtful whether it would contain a section which could go far enough in this respect.

When this point was raised at an extraordinary Annual General Meeting of Chrysler UK, intended to make the company completely US-owned and buy the remaining British-owned shares, it was suggested ASTMS buy Chrysler Corporation shares and go to the company meeting in New York! This response was made replying to one of the authors who was complaining that a legitimate and useful tactic was being withdrawn from the unions.

Social responsibilities?

The second direct effect stems from the lack of social accountability to the people of the country where manufacturing takes place, the threat of withdrawal of investment, a block on new investment or complete closure. In 1970, during the Ford disputes, Henry Ford visited Britain, met the Prime Minister and publicly announced that if the strikes did not end all new investment and a sizeable chunk of the existing operations would be transferred to Spain. In September 1973, Chrysler used a similar threat during a strike of electricians. The Roberts Arundel Company pulled out of Britain completely rather than recognise British trade unions. The cards presently are stacked on the company side. Consider this further: 'resource transfer' can involve single departments; Ford's transferred their design department to Cologne. A Monsanto research department was transferred to Belgium at short notice, and a Shell research department to Holland. What happens to the British employees in these cases, especially in the latter two which have historically been hostile to the concept of staff unionisation? A multi-national company often imports the industrial relations ethic of its country of origin and is more likely to take an anti-union stance than an indigenous British company. Kodak, IBM, Heinz, Shell, Michelin have all been well known for their anti-union policies (although Kodak and Heinz realistically have now come to terms). In Britain one can only place ICI and some insurance companies in their class and, of course, these are all multi-nationals.

131

How can unions cope with the bargaining problems posed by these unpinnable companies? First, by dealing with the information problem and employing research. ASTMS is in the process of dissecting a major single-product multi-national company using British and world-wide contacts, as there is no other way around the problem on a single-union, single-country basis. A great help in this sort of research is the existence of the International Trade Secretariats. There are sixteen of these ranging from the entertainment industry to chemical and metal workers. They have world-wide affiliates and the better ones run solidly-effective information services dealing with comparative employment and profit figures and also estimating investment plans. From such data it is possible to perceive an outline of the multi-national company with the details and colours to be filled later.

International unions

The International Trade Secretariats vary in their effectiveness and ambition. The traditional role of the trans-national trade union organisation has been to seek to organise solidarity in times of dispute and organise the exchange of information; this will no longer be enough. Unions must match the multi-nationals and through these Secretariats, information must become more sophisticated. It may be instructive, briefly, to inspect the structure of one of the most ambitious of these organisations, the International Chemical Workers Federation based in Geneva. The ICF has set up world councils of varying effectiveness, each based on a multi-national company; amongst these are Shell, Michelin, Dunlop-Pirelli, Pilkington-Gobelin, Unilever and Ciba-Geigy. Each world council meets to discuss the prospects of the company in various countries, to attempt to co-ordinate claims and provide for mutual aid. These are new and important departures. It has also developed a European section which is recognised by the EEC for consultation and pre-consultation purposes thereby short-cutting the circuitous route outlined earlier.

The union side, in developing these techniques, is at least in a position to counter some of the corporate moves and in a few notable, if limited, cases, has succeeded. But the whole mechanism is gravely underdeveloped.

In recent times the multi-nationals have been placed in finer focus. There was the case of ITT and its political involvement in Chile during the Allende administration. There followed the extraordinary case of Chrysler threatening to close its entire British operations on the ground that they were unprofitable. This was not to be wondered at, for the company was manufacturing a range of cars of which the most recent was seven years old. It had researched, designed and developed a new car in Britain, yet all the charges for this were set against potential British profits, while the manufacturing is being done in France. This is a typical multi-national tactic. Quite obviously, the unions protested strongly at what they considered to be a commercial manoeuvre which would put 60,000 jobs at hazard. A rescue plan was put into operation with Government backing, but its viability in the longer term remains a matter of some doubt and the facilities still are not secure, simply *because* Chrysler is an insecure multi-national.

As technological advances improve, telecommunications in worldwide situations will make it exceptionally easy for corporate subsidiaries to be manipulated and the multi-national centre will increase its power. The trade union movement will have to organise itself to combat this fact, for if it does not it will be unable properly to represent the rapidly increasing proportion of its members employed by trans-national companies. Use can be made of the trade secretariats, use can be made of the bilateral relationships which many British unions have forged with foreign unions, and use can be made of Government pressures.

As more and more European states legislate for the representation of trades unionists upon the boards of industrial and commercial enterprises, there may be emerging a new situation wherein worker directors may well meet across national frontiers in order to monitor and check the programmes of their companies. If this is done within the trade union framework and on a systematic basis, it could be of immense significance, particularly if the American trades unionists become involved. Clearly the problem is acute in character and growing in size while the trade union response is still ineffective.

Chapter II

Collective bargaining, the Employment Protection Act and other new legislation

'The humblest citizen of the land, when clad in the armour of a righteous cause, is stronger than all the hosts of error.' –
William Jennings Bryan

Prologue

The Conservative Government of 1970–4 earned for the Conservative Party the permanent suspicion of the trade union movement for the enactment of the disruptive Industrial Relations Act which displayed an unknowing hostility to trade unionism, the premises on which it was based and even the structure of collective bargaining. It revived the hostility which had been dampened down since 1939. The Act was based firmly on the restriction and monitoring of free trade union activities and was drafted in a period when it seemed that the entire media had decided to allege that trade unionists were responsible for all the ailments of Britain. This climate has now started to change, as it is realised that this monochrome view was mere camouflage for the whole rainbow of problems which include low investment, poor productivity, dreadful management and an adventuristic stripping of the British industrial base.

When the election of February 1974 saw a Labour Government returned, one of the first demands was for the repeal of the Act, leaving only the Unfair Dismissals provisions in a shortish Trade Union and Labour Relations Act 1974.

There were no mourners for the passing of an Act which sought to greet the decade of the 1970s with the social and moral prejudices of the 1820s. With the removal of that Act there was then a vacuum in industrial relations law which was filled by the passing of the Employment Protection Act in November 1975 after many Parliamentary trials, amended and re-amended clauses, changes of heart and late-night sittings.

This Act had very different objectives to the Industrial Relations Act. Its scope is far more profound, in that it attempts to appreciate the fact that industrial relations encompass not merely an annual confrontation of trade union representatives in bargaining with an employer but embraces the work-task itself, involvement, information and the whole industrial environment. As such, the Act is more of a charter for better industrial relations in that it will, with statutory guidance, remove some of the uncertainties and trigger-points that have stimulated and added to disputes in the past, perhaps not directly, but in their creation of a hostile atmosphere. It is also a straightforward, though belated, move to help employees rather than employers attain rights where none previously existed: it brings Britain further into line with the practices adopted in other countries many years earlier. It may sound carping, yet from the trade union standpoint this Act is not perfect; there are omissions, there are faults, but as a whole it will be an aid to the trade unions in the fight for their members' living standards and their dignity. To criticise on this point; there are many sections which the TUC wanted changed, individual unions wanted changed, and some lawyers specialising in industrial relations wanted changed. The changes were never made and in a host of ways this Act is less favourable to trade unions than the Industrial Relations Act was to employers.

Advisory, Conciliation and Arbitration Service

At the time of writing the Act is not fully operational, in that its practical impact on collective bargaining has yet to be felt. Indeed, some parts of the Act may not be implemented for some time to come; these are the sections requiring ACAS codes of practice and refers to disclosure of information and time off for union activities and education. Nevertheless, it is possible to foresee some of the changes and it is also possible to review the workings of both the unfair dismissals procedure and ACAS, both of which were in existence and working before the enactment. The unfair dismissals procedure is covered elsewhere in this book and suffice to say that the Act both brings the compensation payments up-to-date and adds to the damages for unfair dismissal on the grounds of trade union activity.

The ACAS was set up in September 1974 by the Government prior to the Act, because the passing of the Commission on Industrial Relations (the CIR) with the repealing of most of the Industrial Relations Act left a vacuum which had to be filled. The new Act gives the ACAS a statutory basis and defines its duties and functions quite precisely. Its short history has seen an impressive list of achievements in the settlement of disputes. It has its main functions, as its name accurately suggests, responsibility for advice, conciliation and arbitration on matters which involve industrial relations and its general duties are to improve industrial relations and encourage collective bargaining.

The ACAS employs a team of conciliation officers in its offices around the country and these, if asked by a party to an industrial dispute, will attempt to conciliate or mediate between the parties. There is nothing new in this as such. The Department of Employment had experience of conciliation officers for many years and, indeed, many of these were transferrals to the ACAS. The basic concept of mediation is for a third party to explore the situation and find the common ground, if there is any, between the disputatious factions. It is surprisingly successful in the average dispute, but naturally conciliation is simply a stage in procedure which has to be gone through if there are long-standing and entrenched positions.

The arbitration function has been dealt with elsewhere in this book, although the ACAS must now be added to the list of agencies under whose auspices arbitration can take place.

The ACAS professional staff do not arbitrate themselves. If an application is made to it from one of the parties to the dispute and all the parties agree, the ACAS will, either select an arbitrator or arbiters from a panel that it maintains or, refer it to a new statutory body, the Central Arbitration Committee, which itself will act as the arbiter.

The third function of the service is to advise as and when needed. A whole range of industrial relations matters is involved and it can do this 'on request or otherwise' and the 'otherwise' indicates that it can take the initiative. A non-exhaustive list is given in section 4(2) of the Act and the topics include: organisations of workers, recognition, bargaining and grievance machinery, communications, manpower planning, recruitment and payment systems, in itself a wide range of subjects.

The service has also been charged with the production of Codes of Practice giving 'particular guidance' for 'promoting the improvement of industrial relations'. It has, specifically, to produce Codes on the disclosure of information and on time off for trade union officials and members when engaged on union business. None of the Codes will be legally binding, but may be used in evidence before the CAC, the Industrial Tribunals and the Employment Appeal Tribunal, if applicable.

The Central Arbitration Committee

The CAC is the second of the statutory bodies set up under the Act. Its function as an arbitration board has been mentioned, but it also has other duties. It will take over all the cases referred to the old Industrial Arbitration Board, including Fair Wages Resolution complaints and the new Schedule 11 cases and will be the body to which appeals and complaints under the disclosure of information and recognition provisions can be made.

Independence

One of the main bones of contention, certainly amongst the white-collar unions, in the old Industrial Relations Act, was the way it permitted, and indeed tacitly encouraged, the formation of employer-dominated staff associations and other quasi-unions. There was a definition of an 'independent union', but this was vague and allowed the Registrar of Trade Unions to place almost anyone he chose on the Register, and thus obtain considerable privileges without let or hindrance. Objectors had no standing. Unfortunately the new Act has not put matters right. The definition of independence, which is in the TULRA 1974 and is only marginally better than the Industrial Relations Act definition, still stands despite a late change of heart which saw a Government amendment moved in the Lords, only to see the Leader of the House withdraw it shortly afterwards. A Certification Officer has been appointed and his function is to give a 'certificate of independence' to unions if they meet the requirements of the 1974 Act's definition.

The direct privileges involved are significant and basically revolve around union references to the ACAS or CAC. In all cases, neither body will act on applications from non-certificated organisations. One importance of this relates to the recognition issue. The old Commission on Industrial Relations produced a sensible and comprehensive definition of 'independence' and although it has been ignored, hopefully it can be included by way of an amendment to the Act in the future although this possibility is getting more remote. Elsewhere in the book we have discussed the importance of recognition procedures and the fact that they are of primary importance to trade unions. Without recognition a trade union is gravely inconvenienced and in this context it is a cause for grave concern that the definition of 'independence' is still blurred.

Because of this deficiency a Bill was introduced into the House of Lords by Lord Briginshaw in January 1976. It was a short, two-clause Bill re-defining the word 'independent' as applied to trade unions. It stated that the Certification Officer:

shall in particular take into account the following matters,
a) Any relevant conditions applied by any organisation to which the trade union is affiliated;

b) Whether and to what extent an employer was involved in the establishment of the trade union or continues to be involved in the conduct of its internal affairs;

c) Whether the trade union receives financial or other material support from any employer and the extent of that support and the manner of its provision;

d) Whether meetings held by the trade union are attended by an employer or by representatives of an employer otherwise than by invitation;

e) Whether it is the practice for the trade union to submit minutes of its meetings or to supply other confidential information to an employer;

f) Whether, and to what extent, the policy of the trade union is influenced by an employer otherwise than through the normal processes of collective bargaining;

g) Whether membership of the trade union is confined to employees of a single employer or to employees of associated employers and the effect of such a restriction in the circumstances of the case;

h) Whether the trade union has engaged in collective bargaining with any employer or has shown its intention of doing so.

This Bill, which was drafted with the aid of the ASTMS legal adviser, was supported by the TUC, supported by the Government and was based very firmly on the old CIR criteria. Despite this, it was defeated by the Tory peers on second reading. It is still defective, however, because the criteria are not binding on the Certification Officer, they merely act as a guide.

Subsequently, two Bills were presented in the Commons by Stan Thorne MP. The first of these sought to link the issuing of a Certificate with ACAS by compelling the Certification Officer to take account of good industrial relations. It was withdrawn and replaced by a Bill based on the Briginshaw Amendment but defining TUC affiliation as automatically independent. This fell with the end of the 1975–6 Parliamentary session but was both undefeated and unopposed.

Both the TUC and the Government itself also realise the defectiveness of definition, especially in the light of some of the decisions emanating from the Certification Officer, some of which could only be said to damage good industrial relations. Both the Secretary of State for Industry, in a speech during the report stage of the Shipbuilding Bill and the Minister for Employment in another speech, have indicated the Government's intent to amend the law so as to safeguard good relations by excluding unrepresentative new bodies.

However, the matter is complex and the options many. They range from completely expunging 'independence' from the statute book to issuing an ACAS Code of Practice and giving unions the right to a 'third-party appeal' against the Certification Officer's decision. Although the authors favour the former it is likely that the latter will be the method of choice given the slim Government majority and the hostility of the House of Lords.

The real point is that the post of Certification Officer should never have been created.

ACAS and recognition

The EPA contains a comprehensive recognition section. Trade unions will, as a matter of course, pursue all the normal recognition routines, but in intractable cases an independent union can ask the ACAS to investigate a refusal by an employer to grant recognition under section 11(1) of the Act. The ACAS will investigate the matter using all the traditional means, attitude surveys, discussions or ballots and hopefully will make an award which both sides will accept. The old CIR used to undertake such work and, from time to time, employers such as General Accident, refused to accept the decisions. Indeed, there were two such reports recommending ASTMS as the bargaining agent. By and large the CIR produced reports of the highest quality and built up a good specialist team of industrial relations experts. In the event of such a report being ignored by ACAS, the union involved could apply to the CAC for a legally-enforceable award of terms and conditions of employment as though the union were recognised, only more so, in that normal agreements are not legally enforceable. This is a formidable and subtle penalty and one that most employers will wish to avoid.

There is a form of appeals machinery where either the employer or the union can ask the CAC for the terms to be either amended or revoked. As many of Britain's industrial disputes have taken place over recognition issues, especially in the white-collar field, it is to be hoped that this procedure will lead to a more harmonious acceptance of the realities of industrial life by employers.

At the time of writing, however, the omens are not all good. The delays at ACAS in investigation are substantial and present estimates are that it could take up to two years for a report to be made after the submission of a difficult case. This is partially an understaffing problem, partially a tactical problem. All Section 11 cases have to be submitted to the full conciliation procedure in the first instance, despite the fact that very few of these cases can be resolved in this manner. Some cases have been in conciliation for as long as ten months without the investigation stage even being in sight.

Much of the delay is due to the deliberate procrastination of employers. Although paying lip service to co-operation, they deny ACAS access to employees, raise obstacles to ballots, redefine bargaining areas and invent staff associations. In the face of such hostility, ACAS is powerless except to issue a report based entirely on trade union evidence and attitudes, and this is a procedure which they are reluctant to adopt.

Second, most cases in the regions are being dealt with by non-specialist ACAS staff and this inevitably breeds caution, and thus delay, on their part. The volume of work was hugely under-estimated.

Obviously, such delays tend to compromise a sensitive situation. First, industrial relations are not static and thus the situation as presented in the original case will almost certainly have changed by the time the report is issued. This is obviously unsatisfactory. Second, the mere fact that an ACAS report is being prepared tends to have an effect on activity at the place in question. Postures are struck and attitudes taken, artificial positions are held and the traditional union work slows or even ceases. The longer the delay the greater the disruption and the losers are the employees, though occasionally the employer can find himself in difficulties, too, if harassing action is undertaken.

Information

The Act also confers the right for recognised trade unions to get information from the employer which is necessary for collective bargaining purposes. The Industry Act 1975 also contains information disclosure provisions and Planning Agreement provisions which are partially about longer-term planning information. This right is most important on two levels. The first is that employees should be able to know what the concern they are working for actually does, what its profits are, what its investment is and not just from company accounts, but disaggregated. The problem is this: most large employers are multi-plant and quite often each plant negotiates domestically, as provided for by a national procedure agreement. In such cases the only financial information so far available to a union has been the consolidated group accounts prepared for shareholders whose only concern is the profit as a whole. If the management tells a union that they are losing money, sales are down, and prospects are poor, as they do time after time, there is no adequate short-term gambit the union can deploy to challenge these statements. In any event, the consolidated accounts are generally an inadequate indication of the health of the company. Second, if a union is to pursue a rationally-based claim, it can only do so on the basis of sound information. Industrial relations will be immeasurably improved if companies are not suspected of crying wolf each year as the annual negotiations draw near.

At the time of writing, the Code of Practice has not been issued and so the details of what information may be demanded are not yet known. We know that the Act provides certain exemptions on the grounds of national security, commercial confidentiality and on personal grounds. If an employer refuses to provide the relevant information, an independent, recognised union may apply to the CAC for an order to make the employer disclose. If, after such an order, the employer still refuses, the CAC is empowered, in exactly the same way as with recognition refusal to determine the union claim and this will be legally enforceable.

However a draft Code of Practice prepared by ACAS is circulating on this subject. Although it will probably be amended to some extent the basic provisions are of interest. The Code recommends that 'information agreements' should be negotiated between recognised unions and employers. There are two basic difficulties in this. The first is the multi-union situation where the employers will wish to standardise the information, but the unions themselves may have differing priorities and, indeed, views of the matter. The second is that such an agreement may circumscribe the right to information, especially where a new subject for collective bargaining emerges and this is not covered by the agreement. A clause guaranteeing expansion of information requirements must be added.

The Code, in trying to identify all the bargaining possibilities, suggests that such information (or in the interests of good industrial relations) should come under the following five headings: pay; conditions of service; employment; productivity; financial. Although most of the information is of the standard type, there are some slightly radical suggestions, including proposed organisational and technical changes and transfer pricing. Caution must be expressed as to the effectiveness of this clause and Code until it has been in operation for some time. The reasons for this are not difficult to see. There is no provision in the draft for verifying the accuracy of the information. Second, it is worded such that there is little direct guidance and one can envisage dispute situations arising out of different interpretations.

141

Finally, there is the conceptual problem of the idea itself. The better employer will comply with the Code. However a 'backwoods' employer will have to be taken to the CAC. Yet how can a union argue that the information was needed for collective bargaining purposes if it bargained last year without saying its last settlement was unsatisfactory? As we mentioned earlier the information is for the members, not for the company; they obviously already know it.

These, then are the building blocks for industrial relations contained in the new Employment Protection Act. They will fundamentally affect the nature of trade union work and of employees' responses. There are, however, a great number of other provisions which, although not as basic, none the less are important and affect trade unionists in varying degrees.

The lower paid and the somewhat better off

The first of these is the amendment of Wages Councils arrangements (for poorly-unionised workers) to allow them greater latitude in setting the terms and conditions of service. Ultimately the aim is to get to normal, free collective bargaining but for the present, an intermediary stage of a Statutory Council will be brought into play. For employees who come under the aegis of Wages Councils, this is an excellent development as typically they are amongst the lowest-paid workers in Britain. Alongside this machinery will be an extension of the Terms and Conditions of Employment Act 1959, Schedule 11, which will enable those whose terms and conditions of employment are worse than either the recognised or general level to have claims made on their behalf. Again, this was designed to primarily affect low paid employees, but however, can be used on behalf of those better off.

The part of the Schedule that deals with the 'general level' does not stipulate that the terms and conditions in question have to be negotiated between an employers' association and a union. Although the subsection is confined to the general terms and conditions in a district, it can be used by a union to redress anomalies (especially those created by incomes policies) and also within firms who refuse to recognise a trade union, as well as against a bad employer.

There are two points of interest. The first is that a claim can be made on any condition of service and this could presumably include pensions, holidays, hours of work, etc. The second is that in determining whether or not an award should be made, the CAC must take into account all wages and conditions. In effect, this then becomes an operation on the salary package. In consequence, although the potential benefits are greater the difficulties in establishing a case are multiplied.

All Schedule 11 cases will be channelled through ACAS which will act as a sieve with regard to the appropriateness of the presentation. It is probable that this Schedule, which is outside of incomes policies will play an important role in the coming years.

The CAC may arbitrate on the claims, which in some sense will echo the procedure of the Fair Wages Resolution, but hopefully with less wrangling over definitions and with more satisfactory results for employees. The Fair Wages Resolution is a resolution of the House of Commons. Its aim is to ensure that companies, which have Government contracts, pay their employees the proper rate for the job. The Industrial Arbitration Board which had the duty to adjudicate on references had a mixed record, in that although it has made some awards the majority of cases have foundered on definitions of Government work and comparability of jobs. The CAC have now taken over the adjudication process and to date have adopted a far less legalistic and far more realistic approach. Although both Schedule 11 and the Fair Wages Resolution follow on an older pattern of trying to underpin the weak position of the lower paid their use grows immensely during incomes policies.

Employees' rights

One whole section of the Act is devoted to the 'Rights of Employees'. This is a title embracing a considerable number of disparate ideas. The concepts that have practical implications for collective bargaining are the sections on the rights of employees to have time off from work if they are taking part in trade union activities and for union representatives to carry out union duties. This latter provision is with pay. This also includes time off for educational purposes providing that the course involved will aid the performance of those attending and that it is approved by the TUC or the employees' trade union (providing that it is independent). This is of prime importance to trade unions, and, eventually to employers. It has often been difficult for trade unionists to get the training they need in industrial relations because employers refused to give time off, in spite of the fact that both parties' interests are served by having well-informed bargainers and for the employers not to have to face frustrated officials. Additionally, trade union organisation has often been deliberately thwarted by management's refusing union representatives the time to visit or see other members or hold vital consultative meetings. Once people leave the work-place, it is difficult to contact or assemble them: this section will aid the smooth running of trade unions. It is not a new concept: larger companies have often agreed to pay the salary of someone who is virtually a full-time union official and this practice is spreading through the white-collar sector. The same sections also compel employers to give time off to employees to carry out public duties, such as those undertaken by magistrates, councillors, statutory tribunal members or members of Area and Regional Health Authorities. This has far wider implications outside the scope of collective bargaining, but in short, worker representation on these and similar bodies has often been at a numerically low level due to the fact that the duties are undertaken in working time and employers have refused the time off to attend. The section on union members' rights will be regulated by an ACAS Code of Practice on matters such as how much time off is reasonable and for what activities.

As with the Code on Information, this one is still in a draft stage. The draft, however, is remarkably uninformative and thus not terribly helpful. It is peppered with the word 'reasonable' and not only gives little guidance to either side, but also provides an excuse for employers not to implement the provisions on the grounds that the union involved has been unreasonable.

The draft code recommends that paid time off should be allowed for collective bargaining, meetings with members on the outcome of negotiations (this implies that all union members get time off), meetings with lay officials or other officials on industrial relations business, interviews with members on grievance or disciplinary matters, appearing on behalf of members before outside bodies on industrial relations matters and explanations to new employees on the union.

There is no guidance on the distinction between industrial relations activities and trade union activities beyond suggesting a union company agreement giving a number of days off per period. The code also suggests allowing union members time off to vote in union elections, although no mention of branch meetings. This could lead to a most unsatisfactory state of affairs by denying facilities for one part of an electoral process whilst encouraging another.

Many of the other matters dealt with in the Act do not have a direct effect on collective bargaining, although they do have at least two indirect effects. The first is that they lay down statutory minimum standards for certain benefits, most of which are the subject of negotiation at present and, second, that they remove irritants which have soured relations over the years. We shall mention these in passing.

The first comes into the irritant category, although it has also been the subject of successful negotiations. It is for guaranteed wages in the event of short-time working or lay-offs, unless industrial action by other sections of the work-force have created the circumstances leading to the loss of wages. The proposals are financially modest, although a CBI spokesman, predictably described them as 'ruinous'. The payment is up to a maximum of £6 per day for a maximum of five days (one working week) per quarter. This could amount to a total of £120 per year per employee but is quite unlikely to be reached.

The second provision is for maternity leave and again this is now being widely negotiated, especially in the public service and white-collar areas. Once again the financial provisions are modest and really only set a minimum benchmark from which trade unions will have to progress to avoid the danger of the minimum becoming the maximum. Any worker with two years' employment with the same employer, expecting a child, will be entitled to six weeks' maternity pay and, providing she notifies her intention to return, must be re-employed in the same job at any time up to twenty-nine weeks after the birth. To avoid undue financial hardship on companies or industries employing a large number of younger women, the payments will be made from a new Maternity Pay Fund financed out of employers' National Insurance contributions. Any woman who feels aggrieved by an employer's refusal to provide leave or refusal to reinstate can apply to an Industrial Tribunal and in the latter case, it could be treated as an unfair dismissal. Normally, the woman's trade union will take the case, although she has to make the initial application personally.

One important series of sections, especially in the current economic climate, is that insolvent firms will pay wages or other monies owing to the former employees through the medium of the existing Redundancy Payments Fund. Although this has been a matter for negotiation with Receivers in the past, union efforts to avoid all losses to workers have not always proved totally successful. Employees will also be given longer periods of notice of dismissal. These will be based on a sliding scale dependent upon the number of years worked culminating in twelve weeks' notice after twelve years.

Finally, an employer will have to consult the recognised trade unions and notify the Secretary of State for Employment about impending redundancies. This was explored in chapter seven.

The last provision of this Act to have a more general impact is the setting up of the Employment Appeals Tribunal. This has replaced the High Court in the hearing of appeals from Industrial Tribunals. A judge is chairman and there are two lay members sitting with him. Appeals can only be on points of law and as transcripts are not made in Industrial Tribunals and the chairman's notes would hardly suggest that he himself had misapplied the law, the whole procedure still has to be approached with reserve.

Codes of practice

We have referred to the ACAS Codes of Practice in this and other chapters. At present they are in draft form and are circulating for comments by interested parties. The drafts tend to reflect the composition of the ACAS Council, making partial concessions to the CBI and nods towards the TUC. The results may finally be a compromise which, although ameliorating the differences between the parties, may well not be in the interest of joint industrial relations. The middle way is not always the optimum way in any decision-making process.

Examples of the difficulties are naturally difficult to pinpoint given that the Codes have yet to be published. However, in the Code providing for time off, the TUC wanted some form of list giving guidance to union negotiators and this was the basis of the first Draft. The CBI, however, wished to emphasise the 'permission' element in getting time off, despite the fact that it is now a 'right' in the Act. The first draft has now been re-written taking this point on board. The Code on information provisions has run into the same difficulties in that the CBI, not unnaturally, are attempting to extend the areas which can be regarded as commercially sensitive. Whilst the Codes are not legally binding, they will set standards and hopefully the vision which led to the Act may finally be realised.

It would be neither charitable, nor reflect the importance of this Act, to end this section on that note of disapproval. Without doubt the whole Act will aid the smooth running of industrial relations. Time will tell if the ACAS and the CAC are capable of defusing and settling potentially explosive situations and an even longer time will be needed to see if the provisions affecting the low paid and guaranteed wages make an impact. There are now mechanisms for employers and unions alike to adjust and new rules to learn. In the last analysis all the basic provisions are emollient and unlike its predecessor the 1971 Industrial Relations Act, the 1975 Employment Protection Act should divide few and hopefully mollify the many.

Although the Employment Protection Act is exclusively concerned with conditions of employment and collective bargaining, other recent Acts will have a considerable impact. We have discussed new pensions legislation, the Health and Safety Act, Equal

146

Pay Act and Sex Discrimination Act in the course of this book. The Industry Act and the projected legislation on Industrial Democracy could together or separately radically change the nature of collective bargaining.

Planning agreements

As we have repeated throughout this book, employees and their unions have to react to circumstances on a short-term basis. Not only can this be unsatisfactory in terms of the results which can then be obtained, but it places employees at a disadvantage from the very outset. The Planning Agreement system which is introduced by the 1975 Industry Act, may go some way to reversing this situation. A Planning Agreement is an agreement made by an enterprise or part of the enterprise, with the appropriate Government department concerning its strategic plans for future development. Trade unions will be consulted by the management and by the Government department in the course of working out the Agreement. The Act does not, however, specify this section, nor, at the time of writing has a Planning Agreement been attempted so that the extent of the participation is at best uncertain. Correspondingly uncertain is the actual use of such agreements as they are only voluntary and there is the hazard that only concerns in difficulty may be persuaded to use the new system.

In principle, however, the fact that a union will be able to sit down with management and discuss future manpower requirements, investment intentions, export policies and research projects is a conceptual leap forward. The emphasis then changes from reactive to pre-emptive discussion. In a collective bargaining sense this is a great challenge; in a philosophical sense, where the right of an employee to know what the future may bring is involved, it is long overdue. The system, should it ever become fully operative, will, however, make great demands of trade unions.

The larger companies are all multi-plant, multi-product and probably multi-national. There will be many unions recognised by such a company. The first point is, thus, to set up inter-union committees at plant level, divisional level and group level. The second point is to ensure that the members involved are capable of both understanding and questioning the data. If this is not done, union members could be used as a rubber stamp to legitimise unsatisfactory practices. This will place a great strain on the research and educational facilities of unions, as well as involve a great duplication of effort. A national union planning and research unit as a new major resource centre will have to be considered in such circumstances, given that the subjects will be technical; for example, different forms of investment analysis or market research.

Industrial democracy

If Planning Agreements change the concept of trade union work, then the idea of worker participation, industrial democracy or co-determination will be bound to cause a revolution in attitudes. That there will be legislation is surely without doubt. The Common Market draft Fifth Directive seeks to make employee representation mandatory on supervisory boards. As a result, movements in this direction in member states have all been speeded up.

The Fifth Directive was first drafted by the Commission in 1973 and although devoted to the concept of the harmonisation of the legal framework surrounding limited-liability companies in the EEC, mainly concerned itself with worker participation. It was quite specific on the method by which this should be approached, notably the two-tier board (supervisory and management) system on lines adopted for part of the industry of the Federal Republic of Germany. However, the movement towards such harmonisation was so slow and there was also so much patent 'feet dragging', that a Green Paper was issued on the subject in November 1975. This represented a loosening of the terms of any Directive.

Although worker participation was to remain the 'democratic imperative', the means by which this was to be achieved was left open. Indeed, the Green Paper went so far as to make it clear that a non-legal, non-board body would do, if this had the backing of all concerned. Nevertheless, the ideas in the draft Fifth Directive still stand, binding as to ends, but not as to the means. The concept of the European company, with its worker directors also persists.

Partly because of the pressure put on by these two draft EEC Commission Directives and partly due to the pressure put on by the TUC, outlined in a 1974 report 'Industrial Democracy', a Committee of Enquiry into Industrial Democracy was announced by the British Government in August and set up in December 1975. One of the authors of this book was a member of the Committee. Because of its terms of reference it reported to the Secretary of State for Trade. Its terms of reference were:

Accepting the need for a radical extension of industrial democracy in the control of companies by the means of representation on boards of directors, and accepting the essential role of trade union organisations in this process to consider how such an extension can best be achieved . . . .

148

The Committee Report, in January 1977, right on schedule, just thirteen months after the Committee had first met, was not unanimous. There was a Majority Report signed by the Chairman, Lord Bullock, three trade unionists, two academics and a city solicitor. A Minority Report was presented by the three 'industrialists'. The Majority Report is long and closely argued and plumped for a unitary board with the now famous formula of $2x+y$.

The basic building blocks of the Report are as follows. Any company employing 2,000 or more people will be obliged to accept trade unionists as board members after certain conditions are fulfilled. Whether or not such directors will be appointed will initially be decided by the workforce as a whole in a secret ballot. This must be triggered by an independent union or unions which have recognition on behalf of 20 per cent or more of the workforce. Should the mechanism be triggered the next operation is to decide how large the board will be and to decide on the constituents. It is envisaged that a board of size thirteen would have $5x+5x+3y$. The xs are the union side nominees, whilst the y is made up of people acceptable to both xs. The trade union x must be composed of employees of the enterprise concerned. If there is no agreement on the number, the Report suggests a statutory minimum where $x = 4$ for firms with between 2,000 and 9,999 employees, and up to $x = 7$ for firms employing more than 25,000.

Should there be difficulties in setting either this number, or appointing the y section (to be less than x but more than one) the Industrial Democracy Commission, a new body, will adjudicate. The Commission will also give advice and help to run the ballot on the triggering mechanism. Once the board size is established, the management side appoints their portion (with transitional arrangements for potential supernumery existing directors) and the union side selects their nominees. The exact mechanism for this is left to the unions to decide.

The mechanism through which this will be handled is called the Joint Representation Committee. This will be assembled from the unions involved, at a group level, at an enterprise level, at a company level and at a plant level, that is a pyramidal system of responsibilities. Very similar committees already exist within the trade union movement; Joint Consultative Councils are well established in both the public and private sectors as are Combine Committees. This Committee is responsible for handling the union side negotiations on board size. It may be possible for all the unions concerned to have a seat on the JRC, but it may be necessary for constituencies to be set up which subsume some of the individual unions as obviously there will be problems in multi-union situations. Should disputes occur the matter may be referred to the IDC or the TUC (if all the unions are TUC affiliates).

The selection may be by election or by any other means, but it *must* be done through this single trade union channel. The seats can be divided into separate unions or by constituencies on a single strength basis, or on weighted averages. However, the Majority Report came down heavily against a special seat for senior management on the grounds that such a small percentage of the workforce should not have such a privilege. Management, senior or otherwise, can always participate through trade union machinery, or through the usual job progression channels.

The two xs having been appointed and selected now come together to appoint the y segment. If, after one month, agreement has not been reached, either party can apply to the IDC for either conciliation or ultimately binding nominations.

The ballot for the triggering mechanism would be paid for by the employers, who would also make sufficient facilities available. The IDC, which will have the functions laid out above, in addition to the publication of codes and reports, will be a tripartite body on the lines of ACAS.

Both multi-national corporations and group or holding companies pose problems. The multi-national problem is obvious. Transnational legislation would be needed to provide a group board representation. There are moves afoot for the ETUC to push for EEC legislation requiring EEC based companies to take other EEC national worker directors onto their main boards. However, this is almost certainly further into the future than the implementation of the Bullock Report itself. Basically, the only difference in treatment between the British subsidiary of a foreign-owned multi-national and a domestically-owned company is that in the event of a dispute over the y element, the IDC will appoint after consulting with the parent company and the British Government.

Although there are 750 enterprises employing 2,000 people or more, there are about 1,800 companies. There are also other holding companies which have less than 2,000 employees at head office and less than 2,000 employees in each subsidiary, but which in total employ nearly 20,000 people. There are other holding companies with mixtures of sizes. In cases such as this, flexibility is essential so that choices can be made between the main board or the subsidiaries. The choice will most often depend on what sort of company structure exists, especially regarding the decision-making mechanisms. By and large, the tighter the group control the more essential is main board membership.

These are the proposed mechanisms, but there are other recommendations and observations of some interest. The committee is quite firm on the unitary board principle as opposed to the original TUC evidence, although the TUC gave supplementary evidence which supported the Majority Report. One major problem would be the ability of the shareholders' Annual General Meeting to overrule a board decision. To counter this, the Majority Report has recommended that the board should have the exclusive right to submit resolutions to any AGM on the following matters: dividends, amendments to the articles of association, changes in capital structure, winding up procedures, or the disposal of substantial parts of the enterprise.

The Majority Report then goes on to recommend that the board has the final decision on planning investment, research and development, budgeting (resource allocation), and the payment, appointment and dismissal of management; indeed, it suggests that such recommendations are built into the law.

Confidentiality is a problem, as it is in most collective bargaining areas. There must obviously be the fullest reporting back by worker directors, but equally there will certainly be sensitive data which could harm the enterprise if disseminated. In basic company terms the whole of the report can be summed up by saying that the board must act in 'the best interests of the company' rather than 'the shareholders'. This change is the nub of the whole matter.

There is no guarantee that the proposals in the majority report will be enacted, either in whole or in part. Equally one would suppose that under a Conservative Government there will be no guarantee that the Minority Report would be enacted. What, however, is reasonably certain, is that whilst the UK remains a member of the EEC, we shall have to bring in some form of legislation.

The Bullock Report received a most astonishing reception from the financial press and from the CBI. Rarely has one document been so condemned without due reason being given. Certainly the real challenges and difficulties that would follow implementation of the Majority Report were rarely mentioned.

The difficulties involved, both logistical and legal, should not be underestimated. Nor should the potential changes, both to unions and companies as well as to society as a whole, be belittled. The national British deferential notion that others (generally management) know better, is fast disappearing. However, there is at present no mechanism by which this latent dissatisfaction can be dispelled; employee directors may well provide the appropriate channel.

From the trade union point of view, worker directors extend their bargaining function up to the board room. It does not mean that there will, therefore, be an increase in the numbers of disputes –

far from it. It is that not only is there not always an identity of interest between employees and employers, but that the rule is more often that of conflict. This need not necessarily spill over into hostile words, gestures or actions. It may merely manifest itself as a wariness between the parties based on a mutual suspicion of motives. Given this attitude the representation of British workers on boards may take on a somewhat different character to that practised in either West Germany or Holland.

The unions themselves have two distinct and separate sets of difficulties. The first is to avoid compromising the traditional union functions. It must be apparent to all that negotiating with yourself can be a frustrating and often fruitless exercise. Yet unless care is taken to devise safeguard systems, they may yet occur. Equally, the calibre of the employee directors must be of a high order. It would be only too easy for the shareholder–manager board members to have technical and financial documents presented which lead inexorably to a certain decision; for example, a plant closure without clear decisions being taken on the merits of closure.

The trade union movement will have to grasp this nettle and educate its own membership so that they are capable of critically examining technical arguments and papers. This must be done without their losing the basic union commitment and drive. Some unions, notably the G&MWU, ASTMS, TGWU, NUR and the EEPTU have residential colleges at present, but others will have to follow. One problem has been the lack of finance for such projects as educational establishments are expensive to run and maintain.

In 1976, however, the TUC reversed its previous and long-standing objection to the use of Government monies for educational purposes and as a result are, in the first instance, in receipt of a Department of Education and Science and Department of Employment grant of £400,000. Although a very small sum in relation to the total need, it is a step in the right direction. Most other European countries give trade unions far more than this per year on the impeccable grounds that it is always far better to have a well-informed, professional, trade union movement than one which is technically deficient. £180,000 of this grant is to be allocated to union residential courses and £120,000 to the TUC centrally for tutor training and course development. Compared with Scandinavia or even France, these are small sums but the reimbursement may well make the difference between a good and a mediocre course, or being able to run a course at all.

The courses offered by unions, or by the TUC in their correspondence courses at the central college or in the regions will, because of the new legislation, have to be widened and deepened. Without such changes much of the legislation could prove to be counter-productive as the union members and officials might prove to be hapless approvers. Not only must the new legislation itself be mastered with both the pitfalls and the opportunities explained, but other matters will also have to be taught. Investment analysis, marketing theory, a more than basic economics and corporate planning technique will be needed by those who either have to negotiate planning or participation agreements, or who sit on pension committees or boards of companies. In these instances traditional union strategies cannot prevail, although traditional union attitudes must. It is not a process that seeks to turn trade-unionists into management consultants, but one which will enable them to understand and cut through the jargon which would otherwise debar them from the proper exercise of their duties.

The legislative bundles enacted in 1974, 1975, 1976 and 1977 will, over the next decade, make an enormous impact on collective bargaining. The scope and extent of union activities has been immeasurably enlarged and the opportunities widened. Much of the legislation is enabling in the sense that it will only be as effective as those concerned choose to make it. For the trade union movement this is the time to learn and use the new instruments. Only by so doing will the unions and their members start to realise the potential which they undoubtedly possess, but from which they have been cut off for so long.

Index

154